# 10 YEARS.
# 5 TITLES.
# 1 CLUB.

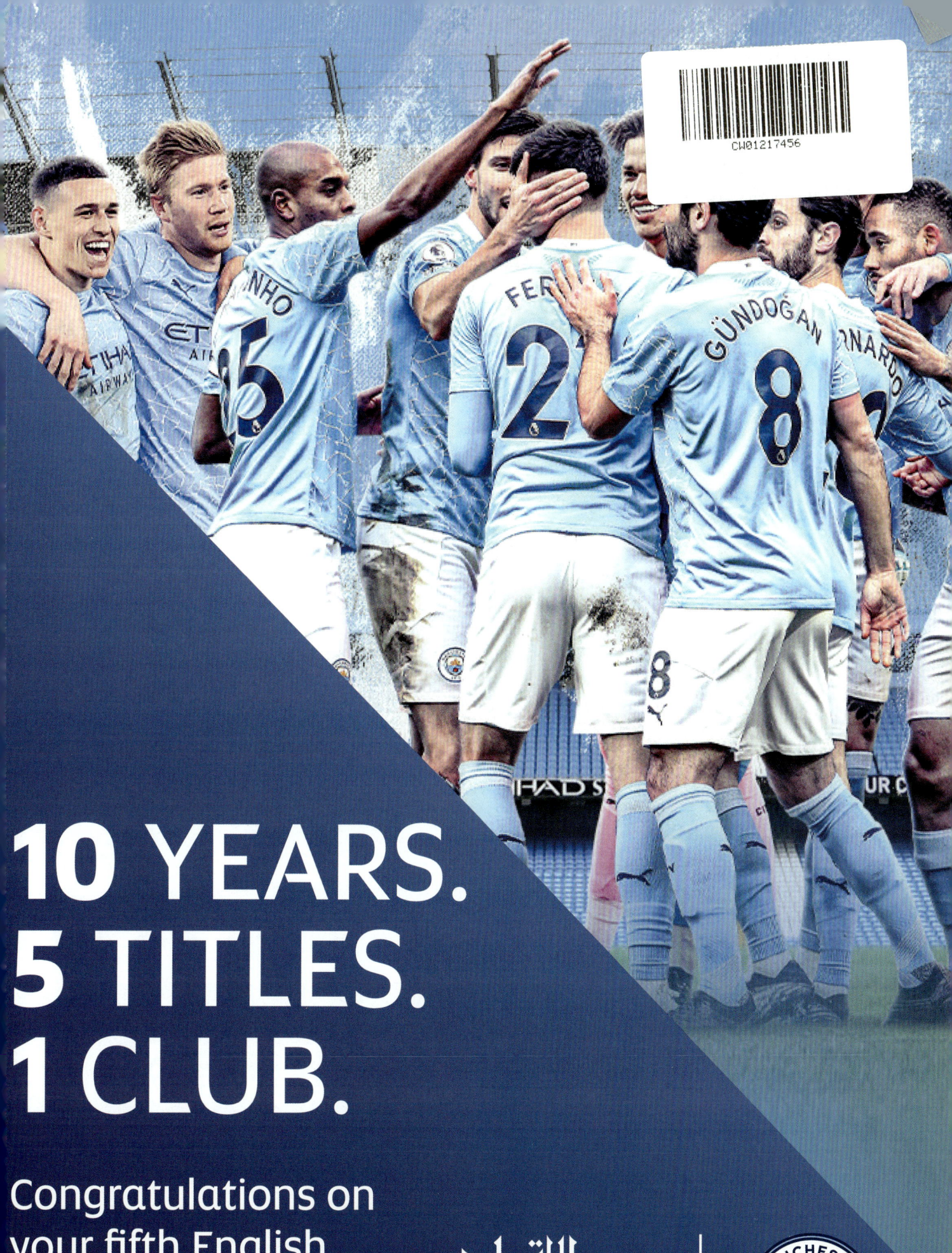

Congratulations on your fifth English Premier League title in 10 years.

ETIHAD AIRWAYS

AT THE EDGE OF THE
WORLD, WHERE THE SKY
SWIMS IN SEA BLUE

this island sanctuary

welcomes you with breeze

and birdsong, candlelit dinners

and infinite views.

Just daydreams away

from the buzz of the capital,

you can lose yourself

in the peaceful luxury

of your own perfect universe.

**AbuDhabi**

YOUR EXTRAORDINARY STORY

Zaya Nurai Island Resort
#InAbuDhabi

visitabudhabi.ae

# CONTENTS

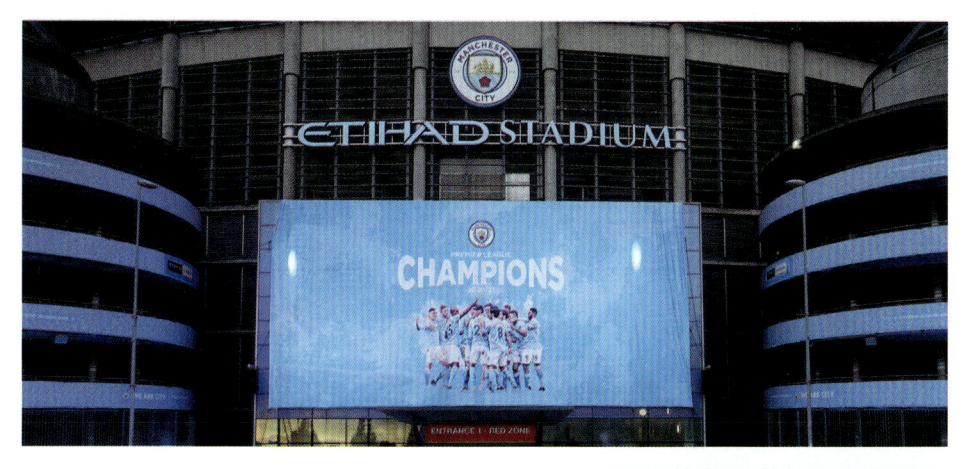

| Page | Section | Description |
|---|---|---|
| 06 | **INTRODUCTION** | Welcome to the story of what has been a sensational season – a season like no other |
| 08 | **PEP GUARDIOLA** | Our proud boss gives thanks after winning his third Premier League title |
| 12 | **FERNANDINHO** | Club captain says it is an honour and a privilege to skipper our champion side |
| 14 | **SERGIO AGUERO TRIBUTE** | Khaldoon Al Mubarak celebrates our departing striker's contribution to the Club |
| 17 | **SEPTEMBER** | Win over Wolves gets season off to a perfect start as title quest begins |
| 22 | **OCTOBER** | Champions League campaign gets underway with impressive wins over Marseille and Porto |
| 28 | **NOVEMBER** | We round off a tough month in style as we put five past Burnley at the Etihad |
| 35 | **DECEMBER** | A busy month – and unbeaten – takes in Champions League, Premier League and League Cup action |
| 42 | **JANUARY** | Invincible City hit their stride and win every game to move top of the Premier League |
| 50 | **FEBRUARY** | Winning run continues at home and abroad as battle continues on four fronts |
| 59 | **MARCH** | The goals flow and records start to tumble as our incredible winning sequence goes on |
| 67 | **APRIL** | The first trophy of the season is in the bag as we extend our lead at the top of the Premier League |
| 76 | **MAY** | City rivals' defeat confirms Premier League title after ticket to Champions League final is booked |
| 84 | **PICTURE PERFECT** | A look back at an incredible season through the eyes of our award-winning photographers |
| 92 | **NEXT GENERATION** | Premier League success for EDS and Under-18s gives us an unprecedented hat-trick of titles |
| 94 | **RECORD BREAKERS** | A deep dive into the facts and figures behind our record-breaking season |

## MANAGEMENT

Director of Football
**TXIKI BEGIRISTAIN**

Head Coach
**PEP GUARDIOLA**

Assistant Coach
**JUAN MANUEL LILLO**

Assistant Coach
**BRIAN KIDD**

Assistant Coach
**RODOLFO BORRELL**

Head of goalkeeping
**XABIER MANCISIDOR**

Goalkeeper coach
**RICHARD WRIGHT**

Head of Academy
**JASON WILCOX**

Under-23 EDS manager
**ENZO MARESCA**

Under-23 GK coach
**ANDY MULLINER**

Under-18 Academy Team Manager
**CARLOS VICENS**

Under-18 GK coach
**MAX JOHNSON**

Chief scout
**CARLO CANCELLIERI**

Women's Managing Director
**GAVIN MAKEL**

Women's Head coach
**GARETH TAYLOR**

**MANCHESTER CITY**
Senior Licensing Manager
Gavin Johnson
Written Content Lead
Robert Pollard

**PUBLISHED BY REACH SPORT**
Production Editor Nick Moreton
Designers Colin Harrison, Lee Ashun
Managing Director Steve Hanrahan
Senior Executive Art Editor Rick Cooke
Executive Editor Paul Dove
Commercial Director Will Beedles
Marketing & Communications Manager Claire Brown

**PHOTOGRAPHY**
Getty Images, Victoria Haydn, Matt McNulty, Tom Flathers/Manchester City FC via Getty Images

**PRINTED BY** Buxton Press

---

Football League First Division Premier League champions:
**1936/37, 1967/68, 2011/12, 2013/14, 2017/18, 2018/19, 2020/21**

Football League First Division Premier League Runners-up:
**1903/04, 1920/21, 1976/77, 2012/13, 2014/15, 2019/20**

FA Cup winners:
**1903/04, 1933/34, 1955/56, 1968/69, 2010/11, 2018/19**

FA Cup Runners-up:
**1925/26, 1932/33, 1954/55, 1980/81, 2012/13**

Football League Cup winners:
**1969/70, 1975/76, 2013/14, 2015/16, 2017/18, 2018/19, 2019/20, 2020/21**

Football League Cup Runners Up:
**1973/74**

UEFA Champions League Runners-up:
**2020/21**

European Cup Winners' Cup winners:
**1969/70**

FA Charity Shield / FA Community Shield winners:
**1937, 1968, 1972, 2012, 2018, 2019**

FA Charity Shield / FA Community Shield Runner-up
**1934, 1956, 1969, 1973, 2011, 2014**

Second Division / First Division / Championship Winners
**1898/99, 1902/03, 1909/10, 1927/28, 1946/47, 1965/66, 2001/02**

U23s Premier League 2 Winners:
**2020/21**

U18s FA Youth Cup Winners:
**1986, 2008, 2020**

FA Womens Super League 1:
**2016**

FA Women's Cup:
**2016/17, 2018/19, 2019/20**

FA WSL Continental Cup:
**2014, 2016, 2018/19**

www.mancity.com 05

PREMIER LEAGUE CHAMPIONS 20/21

# A season like no other
## City to the fore in record-breaking campaign

HELLO and welcome to this special commemorative Champions magazine.

It's been a sensational season for Manchester City Football Club.

Pep Guardiola's team continue to impress with a wonderful brand of attacking football that has seen us become the preeminent side in English football.

In April, we secured our fourth-successive League Cup triumph, beating Tottenham in a hard-fought final, with Aymeric Laporte's header enough to separate the sides.

And little more than two weeks later, our third Premier League title in four years was confirmed.

City have now collected 10 of the last 15 major English trophies available, a figure that underlines our consistency and quality over a sustained period.

But it's perhaps the manner in which we secured those trophies that has impressed the most. We have set a series of significant records along way, which are laid out in more detail on pages 94-97, including a new Premier League record for the longest sequence of wins from the start of a calendar year (13) and a remarkable run of 21 consecutive victories in all competitions between December and March, another English football record.

There has also been significant improvement in the UEFA Champions League, too, as we made it to our first final of Europe's elite knock out tournament.

Against the backdrop of the global health pandemic, to show such consistency has been extraordinary, with Guardiola's ability to innovate and adapt key to our story of success.

Of course, we had all hoped that the final glorious chapter of the season would be written in Porto after securing a place in our first ever Champions League final when we beat Paris Saint-Germain 4-1 on aggregate in the semi-finals.

We had won 11 and drawn one of our Champions League matches going into the final, but it was an unlucky 13th game

INTRODUCTION

for Pep Guardiola and his Premier League Champions in Porto on May 29.

While a 1-0 defeat at the Estadio do Dragao was hugely disappointing, this has been one of the finest seasons in the club's 127-year history - and our success hasn't been confined simply to the first team.

Our EDS won the Premier League 2 and our U18s were crowned U18s Premier League National champions, meaning City are the first club to win a hat-trick of Premier League titles in the same season - a magnificent accomplishment that demonstrates the strength of our organisation at every level.

Indeed, Enzo Maresca's EDS dominated their division, finishing the campaign 14 points ahead of our nearest challengers.

For Carlos Vicens' U18s, it was a little tighter, with a final-day win at Burnley seeing us leapfrog second-placed Manchester United to finish top of the U18s Premier League North, before a superb 3-1 over Fulham in the National final.

Two other major pieces of silverware, which had rolled over from the 2019/20 season due to COVID-19 pandemic, were secured in November as we lifted the Women's FA Cup for the third time in four seasons and the FA Youth Cup for the first time since 2008.

However, in amongst those magnificent moments, we lost a club legend. Colin Bell passed away peacefully in January after a short, non-Covid related illness, aged 74.

He is widely regarded to be the finest City player of his generation, making 501 appearances and scoring 153 goals for the Club during a 13-year stay.

Few players have left such an indelible mark on City. He would no doubt have been proud of the success the club has had this season.

And we want to say a huge thank you to all our fans. During a difficult period for the whole world, you haven't been able to watch us up close, but your support from afar has meant everything to players and staff across the club. Our achievements this season are for you.

www.mancity.com

**MANAGER'S NOTES**

# So proud of this special Club

**HI everyone, I hope you're well.**

What a pleasure it is to be able to write to you having won the Premier League title again – our third in four seasons. Given how many top teams are in this league, to be so consistent is amazing and testament to the quality of my players.

This has been a season and a Premier League campaign like no other, the hardest one, no doubt about that. The Premier League is the most important title for us. It's the one where you have to be there every three days, playing all your rivals home and away. Only by being the very best, week in week out, can you win this competition. It is a huge success to have won it again.

Believe me, I have managed in Spain and Germany before coming here, and this is the hardest one. And the toughest period is the winter time, when the games are relentless and the weather brings extra difficulties. The fact we won all our games around that period is amazing and is the reason we have ended up as champions.

I am so proud to be the manager of this squad. The players are special.

08 www.mancity.com

www.mancity.com 09

**PREMIER LEAGUE CHAMPIONS 20/21**

To come through this season – with all the restrictions and difficulties we've faced – and show the consistency we have is remarkable. Every single day, they are there, fighting for success, trying always to be better. They have adapted to every situation and difficulty they have faced. It's been remarkable to be part of it.

We could not do what we have done without the backroom staff. They are the best around - consummate professionals who love football and want the best for Manchester City.

Not forgetting, of course, all the staff across our organisation who work to make this club the success it is. Whether that's been from the offices at CFA or working from home, the efforts of every employee in such trying circumstances have contributed to this achievement.

And Khaldoon is the perfect chairman. I spoke with him in November, and he convinced me to stay here longer. The trust between us is strong and I have always felt his support, even in the difficult times. When I was here in the first season, I didn't win anything but the support I had from the Chairman has never changed. It is so important for a manager to have that encouragement and I am so grateful to him for everything he has done for me.

I want to say a huge thanks to all our fans. We appreciate your support so much.

> "WE SENSE YOUR LOVE, WE APPRECIATE IT AND WE COULD NOT HAVE DONE WHAT WE HAVE DONE WITHOUT IT"

# MANAGER

In our toughest moments, we couldn't hear you inside the stadium, but we know you are with us everywhere we go and that has lifted us.

I promise you we sense your love, we appreciate it and we could not have done what we have done without it.

This one is really for our fans – and especially for Colin Bell and all his family. We lost a legend during the season and it affected everyone inside the club. I think this Premier League title would make him proud.

Thank you for your continued support!

## PEP GUARDIOLA TOTAL TROPHIES

| COMPETITION | WON |
|---|---|
| **MANCHESTER CITY** | |
| PREMIER LEAGUE | 3 |
| FA CUP | 1 |
| LEAGUE CUP | 4 |
| COMMUNITY SHIELD | 2 |
| **BAYERN MUNICH** | |
| GERMAN BUNDESLIGA | 3 |
| DFB-POKAL | 2 |
| FIFA CLUB WORLD CUP | 1 |
| UEFA SUPER CUP | 1 |
| **BARCELONA** | |
| SPANISH LA LIGA | 3 |
| COPA DEL REY | 2 |
| SPANISH SUPER CUP | 3 |
| CHAMPIONS LEAGUE | 2 |
| SUPER CUP | 2 |
| CLUB WORLD CUP | 2 |
| TOTAL | 31 |

## PEP GUARDIOLA MAN CITY STATS TOTALS 2016/21

| COMPETITION | PLAYED | WINS | DRAWS | LOSSES | GOALS FOR | GOALS AGAINST |
|---|---|---|---|---|---|---|
| PREMIER LEAGUE | 190 | 140 | 23 | 27 | 465 | 156 |
| LEAGUE CUP | 25 | 19 | 4 | 2 | 55 | 15 |
| FA CUP | 25 | 20 | 1 | 4 | 70 | 14 |
| CHAMPIONS LEAGUE | 52 | 35 | 7 | 10 | 120 | 54 |
| TOTALS | 292 | 214 | 35 | 43 | 711 | 239 |

www.mancity.com 11

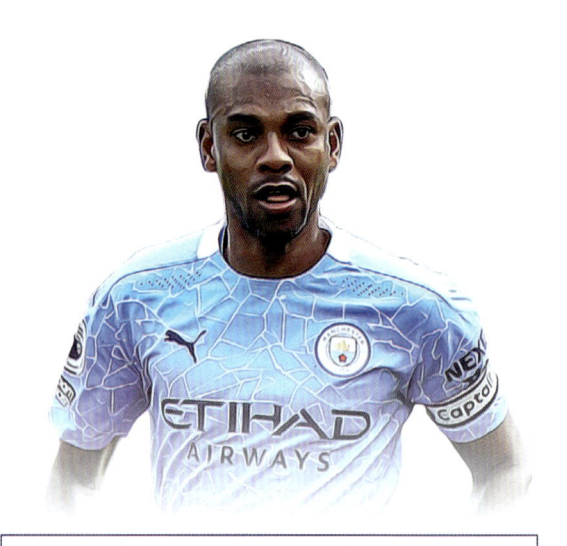

## CAPTAIN'S NOTES

# We did it together

**HELLO City fans! First of all, I want to say a big THANK YOU from all the players and staff. Your support this season has been amazing, even though you haven't been able to be with us inside the stadium. We see and hear your messages and they mean so much to us. It is an honour to play for you and we hope we have made you happy with the way we have performed on the pitch.**

I am so proud and so happy with what we have achieved this season. The Premier League is the hardest league in world football – every single game is tough. We can't hide at any stage; we have to show fight every single game to be successful. Mentally and physically it's tough, so to win the league again means the world to me and the rest of the squad.

It's particularly satisfying this year, given the difficulties we have faced. We all know what has happened across the world. It's been an incredibly hard period for everyone. Hopefully things can return to normal soon and we can start seeing our fans regularly at the Etihad again.

Winning the Premier League title is the ultimate fulfilment of a player's ambition. It's what we all dreamed of as young boys, so to do it is a wonderful feeling. I dreamt to win as many titles as possible when I signed here. I made the right choice when I decided to join Manchester City!

To captain this team is an honour and a privilege because the players have given their all throughout the season, whether in training or in matches. I can honestly say, it's one of the best groups of people I've worked with and we consider each other as family, we sacrifice so many things to reach our goals. It's something I will never forget.

The teamwork has been amazing. We are a group of players who show togetherness and fight day in, day out. Football is everything to us and we strive every single day to be as good as we can be in the hope we can bring success to Manchester City.

And we could not do any of it without the amazing staff behind us. Pep and his backroom team provide everything we need to perform on the pitch. We have the best medical team, support staff, chefs, masseurs, kitmen…everyone has played a vital role in helping us secure the title.

Winning the Premier League so soon after lifting the Carabao Cup is our reward for all the hard work we've put in.

Rest assured we will continue to do everything we can to bring more trophies home for you and this amazing club next season.

Thank you so much for your love and support.

www.mancity.com 13

PREMIER LEAGUE CHAMPIONS 20/21

# CHAIRMAN'S FAREWELL TO LEGEND KUN

**AFTER 10 wonderful years we are saying farewell to Sergio Aguero, a player whose impact on City, the fans and football in England cannot be overstated.**

The description legend can easily be overused or be an exaggeration but in Sergio's case this is clearly not so. Having won 15 titles in his time with us, he is the most decorated player in the long, proud history of this football club.

His influence and input on the field is indelibly etched into the fabric of Manchester City and the sport itself.

Sergio has earned his place in the pantheon of Premier League all-time greats and in the affection of all City fans wherever they may reside.

Even if you only have time for a cursory glance at his statistics over the past decade, Sergio's record has been phenomenal.

Nearly 400 appearances and more than 250 goals figures that speak for themselves but they are by no means the whole story.

On May 13th, 2012 Sergio produced one of sport's greatest ever moments when he scored the emotional title winning goal against Queens Park Rangers. Whilst that is the most famous of all his City goals and moments it is just a small part of Sergio's City journey.

His zest for life, his infectious personality, and his loyalty over the past 10 years have been inspirational. He has motivated and moved a whole generation of City fans all over the globe.

FAREWELL SERGIO

**"WE HAVE ALREADY ANNOUNCED THAT WE HAVE COMMISSIONED A STATUE OF SERGIO - THAT WILL STAND ALONGSIDE THOSE OF DAVID SILVA AND VINCENT KOMPANY OUTSIDE THE ETIHAD STADIUM"**

He has been an exceptional striker but also an exceptional human being to have within our number, first at Carrington and then the CFA. Whilst he put fear into opposition defenders, he filled his many colleagues and friends with nothing but joy and appreciation.

Sergio, like David Silva before him, did most of his talking on the pitch but make no mistake in his way he was also a leader – by example.

We have already announced that we have commissioned a statue of Sergio - that will stand alongside those of David Silva and Vincent Kompany outside the Etihad Stadium as a testament to his and their brilliance and personalities - it is well merited.

We part company with Sergio with the highest respect, and great warmth and the affection. We wish him nothing but success and happiness at Barcelona and for him to be secure in the knowledge that he will always part of this City family.

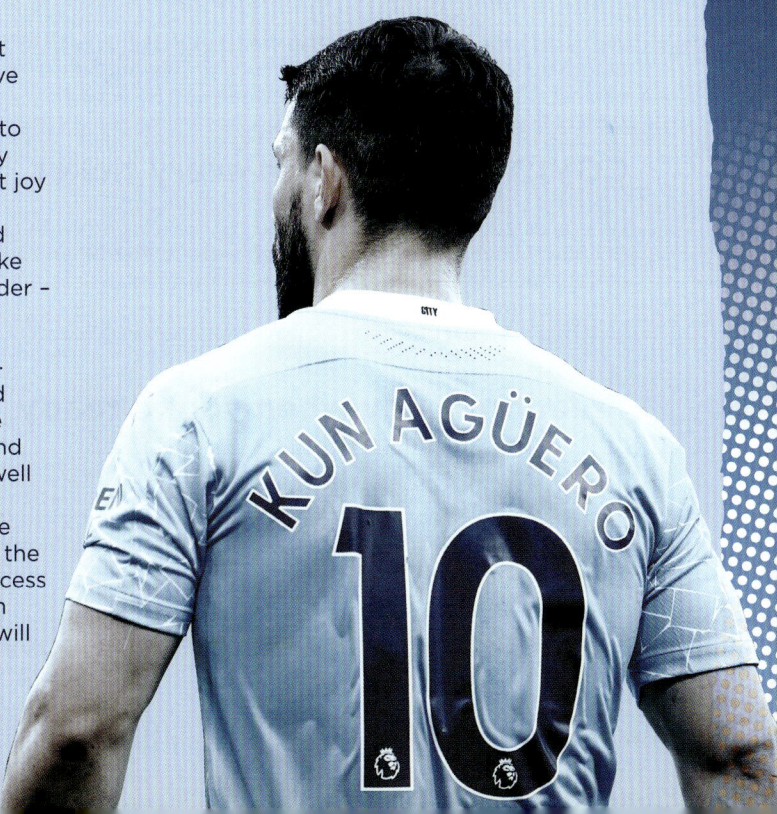

# Reclaim the summer...

**It's time to reclaim the summer. Make up for lost time with friends and family or just get lost somewhere new. When you're ready to start flying again, book your well-deserved trip with Etihad Airways for flexibility, more choice and total peace of mind.**

**We're flying to more than 60 worldwide destinations and have introduced new measures to keep everyone safe, comfortable and protected when they travel. You can even change your flight for free if you need to.**

**And after Man City did the double in claiming the Carabao Cup and Premier League victories this year, there's never been a better time to celebrate.**

## Your wellness, our priority

We understand how important is for you and your family to feel safe and comfortable when you travel. With Etihad Wellness and a team of Wellness Ambassadors on hand 24/7, we'll keep you protected at every step of your journey.

All of our aircraft are deep cleaned at every destination, and our HEPA filters on board remove 99% of microbes in the air – because cleaner air means cleaner cabins.

We're also the only airline in the world to make COVID-19 PCR testing mandatory before every flight, and all of our crew and pilots on board have been vaccinated against COVID-19. You'll feel safe when you fly with us.

## COVID-19 cover with every ticket

Wherever you choose to fly to, you can travel there with confidence thanks to global COVID-19 cover. If you're diagnosed with COVID-19 whilst you're away, we'll take care of your medical expenses and quarantine costs.

Included with every Etihad Airways ticket when you travel before 31 September 2021.

## Freedom to fly when you're ready

Sometimes, plans change. And that's ok.

We're allowing unlimited changes on all new bookings to give you more freedom and flexibility. Book today and change your flight for free later if you need to. Simple.

### Visit etihad.com/wellness to discover more.

**ETIHAD AIRWAYS**

SEPTEMBER

# City maul
## Wolves in their own lair
De Bruyne gets season off to perfect start

PREMIER LEAGUE CHAMPIONS 20/21

CITY made the perfect start to the 2020/21 Premier League season with a fine 3-1 win away at Wolves.

A superb first 45 minutes proved crucial as the we took the game to the hosts from the off and we made a deserved breakthrough on 20 minutes through Kevin De Bruyne's penalty, after the Belgian had been brought down in the box.

Twelve minutes later we doubled our lead when Phil Foden rounded off a stunning move with a fine side-footed finish.

Wolves rallied after half-time and things got tense when Raul Jimenez struck 12 minutes from time, before Gabriel Jesus wrapped up the points with the last kick of the game.

21.09.20
Molineux Stadium, Premier League

**WOLVES**   1
Jimenez (78)

**MAN CITY**   3
De Bruyne (pen 20) Foden (32) Jesus (90)

21.09.20
Etihad Stadium, Carabao Cup

**MAN CITY**   2
Delap (18) Foden (75)

**BOURNEMOUTH**   1
Surridge (22)

27.09.20
Etihad Stadium, Premier League

**MAN CITY**   2
Riyad Mahrez (4) Nathan Ake (84)

**LEICESTER CITY**   5
Vardy (pen 37, 53, pen 58)
Maddison (77) Tielemans (pen 88)

30.09.20
Turf Moor, Carabao Cup

**BURNLEY**   0

**MAN CITY**   3
Sterling (35, 49) Torres (65)

18 www.mancity.com

SEPTEMBER

# Dream Delap debut

## LIAM DELAP PERSONAL STATS

| DATE OF BIRTH | PLACE OF BIRTH | POSITION | MAN CITY DEBUT |
|---|---|---|---|
| 8TH FEBRUARY 2003 | WINCHESTER | CENTRE FORWARD | v BOURNEMOUTH CARABAO CUP 24.09.20 |

Three days later, 17-year-old Liam Delap scored on his debut as the holders reached the fourth round of the Carabao Cup with a 2-1 win over Bournemouth.

The striker, one of five teenagers to start in a much-changed and youthful City side, put the hosts ahead with a powerful drive.

Bournemouth levelled after a smart turn and shot from Sam Surridge beat our other debutant Zack Steffen, but with a penalty shootout looming large, the impressive Phil Foden, who was the architect of much of our best play, sent us through with a tap in after Riyad Mahrez's effort came back off the post.

www.mancity.com 19

PREMIER LEAGUE CHAMPIONS 20/21

There was disappointment the following Sunday as our first home game of the campaign ended with a heavy loss to Leicester.

Despite taking an early lead through Leicester old boy Riyad Mahrez, the visitors managed to get in behind the City defence on a number of occasions and when they did, they invariably punished some hesitant defending.

The Foxes were awarded three penalties, Jamie Vardy bagging a hat-trick in the 5-2 loss. Nathan Ake headed Kevin De Bruyne's corner home on 84 minutes, but it was no more than a consolation for a very off-colour City side in what was our first opening home game defeat in the top flight since 1989.

**WE ARE NOT GOING TO CREATE 10 CHANCES. WE HAVE TO KNOW IT IS DIFFICULT. EVEN AT 5-2 LEICESTER WERE IN THE 18-YARD BOX. I AM NOT GOING TO GIVE UP, I AM GOING TO TRY TO FIND SOLUTIONS**

PEP GUARDIOLA

## Goodbye Nicolas Otamendi

**September marked the end of an era for City stalwart Nicolas Otamendi, as the Argentine defender departed for pastures new.**

The 33-year-old defender set off to embark on a new challenge with Benfica in Portugal after five years of fantastic service, during which he helped the Club lift every major honour in the English game.

In total, Otamendi made 210 appearances, scoring 11 goals and he departed as a two-time Premier League champion, with four League Cup medals to his name and having lifted the FA Cup in 2019.

He also won the Community Shield on two occasions.

### NICOLAS OTAMENDI PERSONAL STATS

| DATE OF BIRTH | PLACE OF BIRTH | POSITION | MAN CITY CAREER | ARGENTINA CAREER |
|---|---|---|---|---|
| 12TH FEBRUARY 1988 | BUENOS AIRES, ARGENTINA | CENTRE BACK | 210 APPEARANCES, 11 GOALS | 74 APPEARANCES, 4 GOALS |

**SEPTEMBER**

It was then back to the Carabao Cup and defending champions City bounced back to form with a comprehensive 3-0 win over Burnley to move into the quarter-finals.

Ferran Torres scored his first goal for the club to wrap up a comfortable victory that a dominant City thoroughly deserved, after Raheem Sterling's brace had put us in a commanding position at Turf Moor.

Sterling fired home the opener from 10-yards after being picked out with a good ball from Benjamin Mendy and City's second came down the same flank when Torres cut back for City's No.7 to score from close range.

The Spaniard looked lively throughout and when Riyad Mahrez's through ball put him clear of the Burnley defence, he calmly curled the ball into the bottom corner to get up and running in a City shirt.

www.mancity.com

PREMIER LEAGUE CHAMPIONS 20/21

# Sterling
## performance
Raheem enjoys heat of the battle

OCTOBER

**TWO sides known for an intense, free-flowing style of play certainly did not disappoint in an exciting 1-1 draw in West Yorkshire.**

Raheem Sterling opened the scoring just before the 20-minute mark when he tiptoed his way into the box from the left before whipping the ball through a crowd of bodies and into the far corner.

But the England winger's opener was cancelled out just before the hour mark by Leeds substitute Rodrigo, who reacted quickest when the ball dropped invitingly inside the box from a corner.

A breathtaking game continued to ebb and flow with both sides creating chances on a wet and windy evening at Elland Road.

**THEY WERE RIGHT IN OUR FACES. I PREFER PLAYING AGAINST TEAMS LIKE THAT INSTEAD OF 11 MEN BEHIND THE BALL. IT WAS A DIFFICULT GAME. THE ENERGY LEVELS FROM START TO FINISH WERE IMPRESSIVE** RAHEEM STERLING

www.mancity.com 23

# 100% OF OUR CREW ARE VACCINATED

We're the first airline in the world to vaccinate all pilots and cabin crew on board against COVID-19.

etihad.com/wellness

ETIHAD
AIRWAYS

OCTOBER

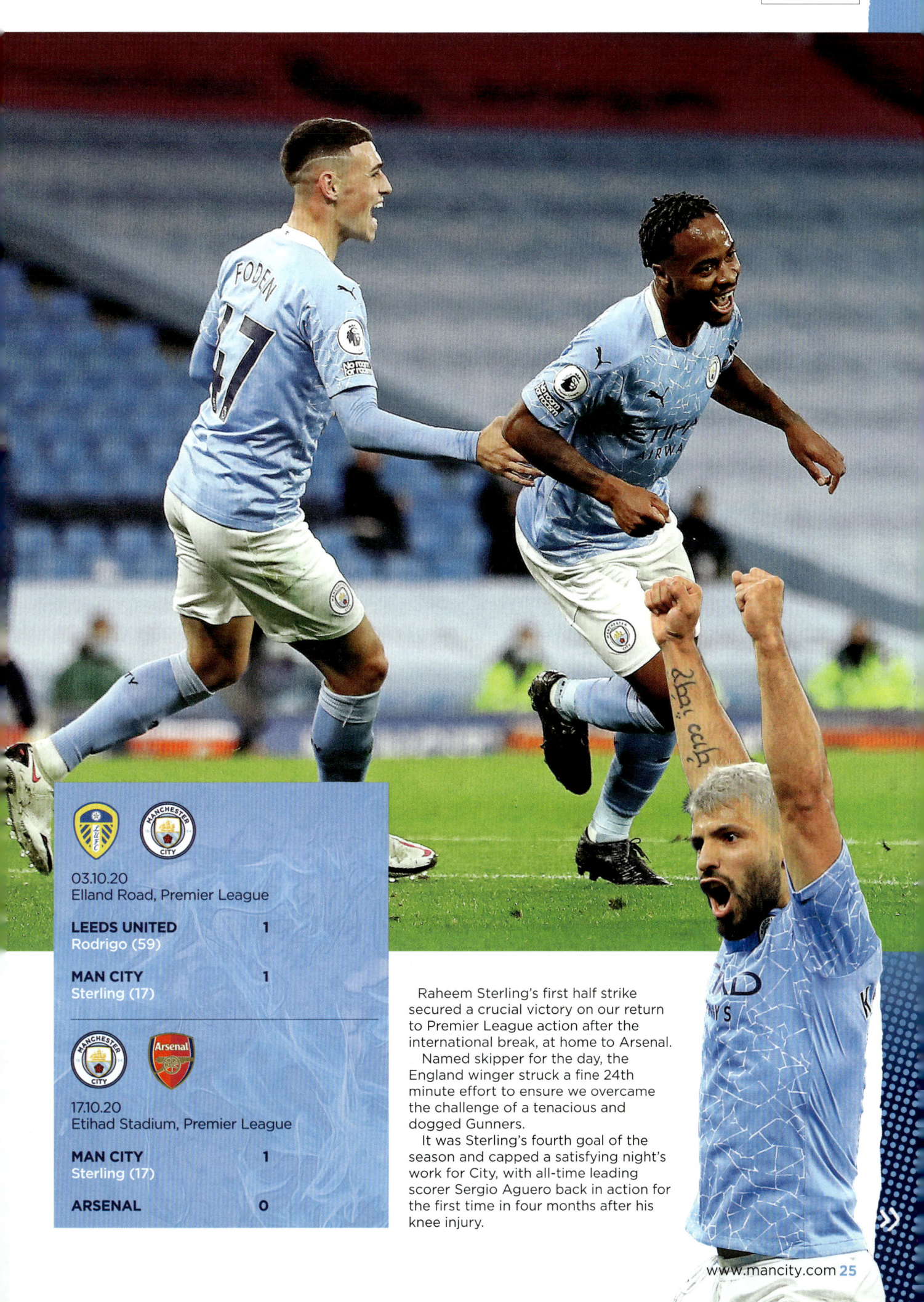

03.10.20
Elland Road, Premier League

**LEEDS UNITED**   1
Rodrigo (59)

**MAN CITY**   1
Sterling (17)

---

17.10.20
Etihad Stadium, Premier League

**MAN CITY**   1
Sterling (17)

**ARSENAL**   0

Raheem Sterling's first half strike secured a crucial victory on our return to Premier League action after the international break, at home to Arsenal.

Named skipper for the day, the England winger struck a fine 24th minute effort to ensure we overcame the challenge of a tenacious and dogged Gunners.

It was Sterling's fourth goal of the season and capped a satisfying night's work for City, with all-time leading scorer Sergio Aguero back in action for the first time in four months after his knee injury.

www.mancity.com 25

**PREMIER LEAGUE CHAMPIONS 20/21**

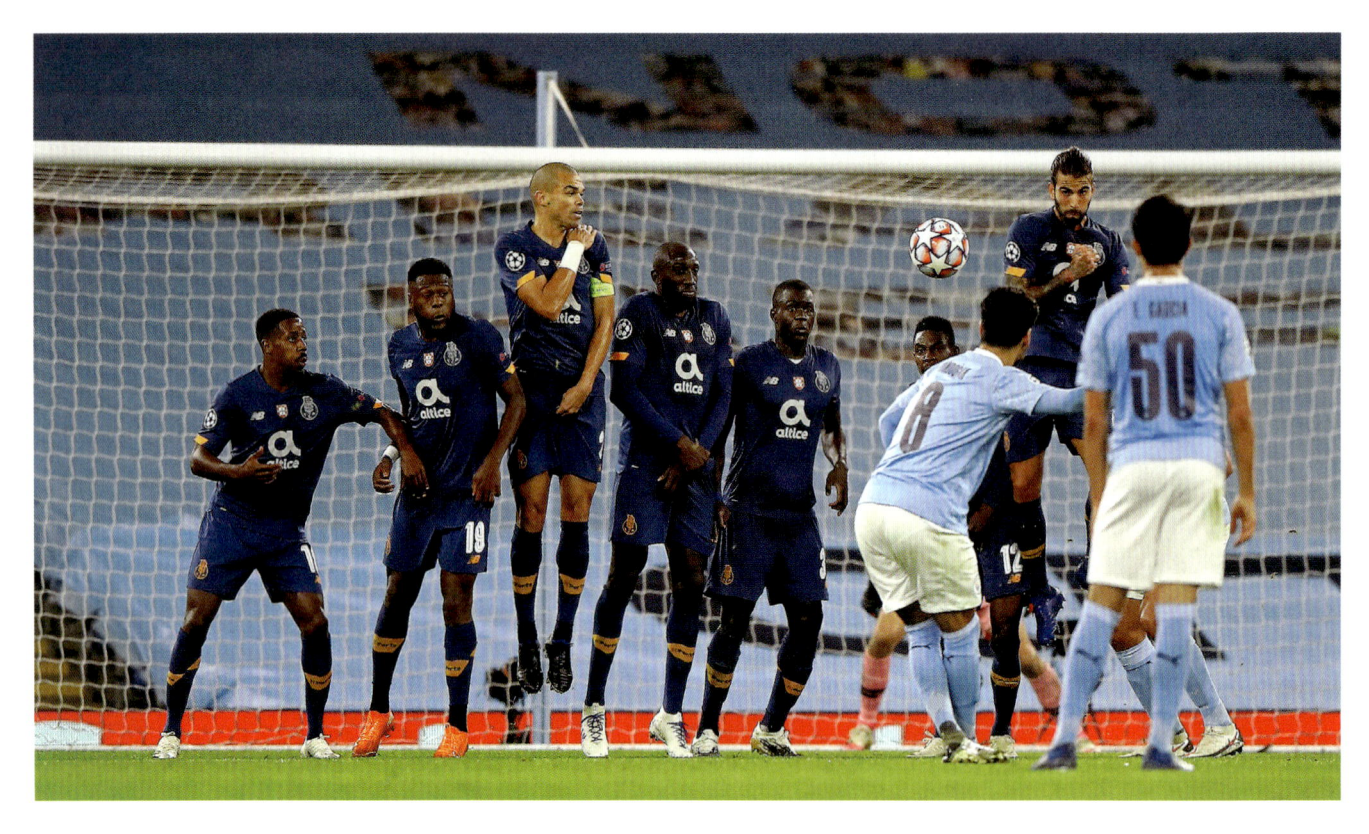

City's Champions League campaign got off to a fine start with a 3-1 win over Porto at the Etihad.

The visitors took an early lead, but we fought back with a quick leveller from Sergio Aguero and second-half strikes from Ilkay Gundogan and Ferran Torres completed what, ultimately, was a comfortable win.

For Riyad Mahrez and Raheem Sterling, the night took on added significance, the Algerian making his 100th appearance for the Club and Sterling clocking up his 250th game in a City shirt.

City were forced to settle for a point as we drew 1-1 against a stubborn West Ham United at the London Stadium.

Pep Guardiola's side came from behind to claim a share of the spoils, with man-of-the-match Phil Foden's smart turn and shot levelling the scores after Michail Antonio had put the hosts ahead with a superb overhead kick.

The Hammers had edged the first half, but City completely dominated after Foden's equaliser and might have won it late on only for Lukasz Fabianski to deny Raheem Sterling and Riyad Mahrez, in a game in saw both Ederson and Kyle Walker notch up 150 appearances for the Club.

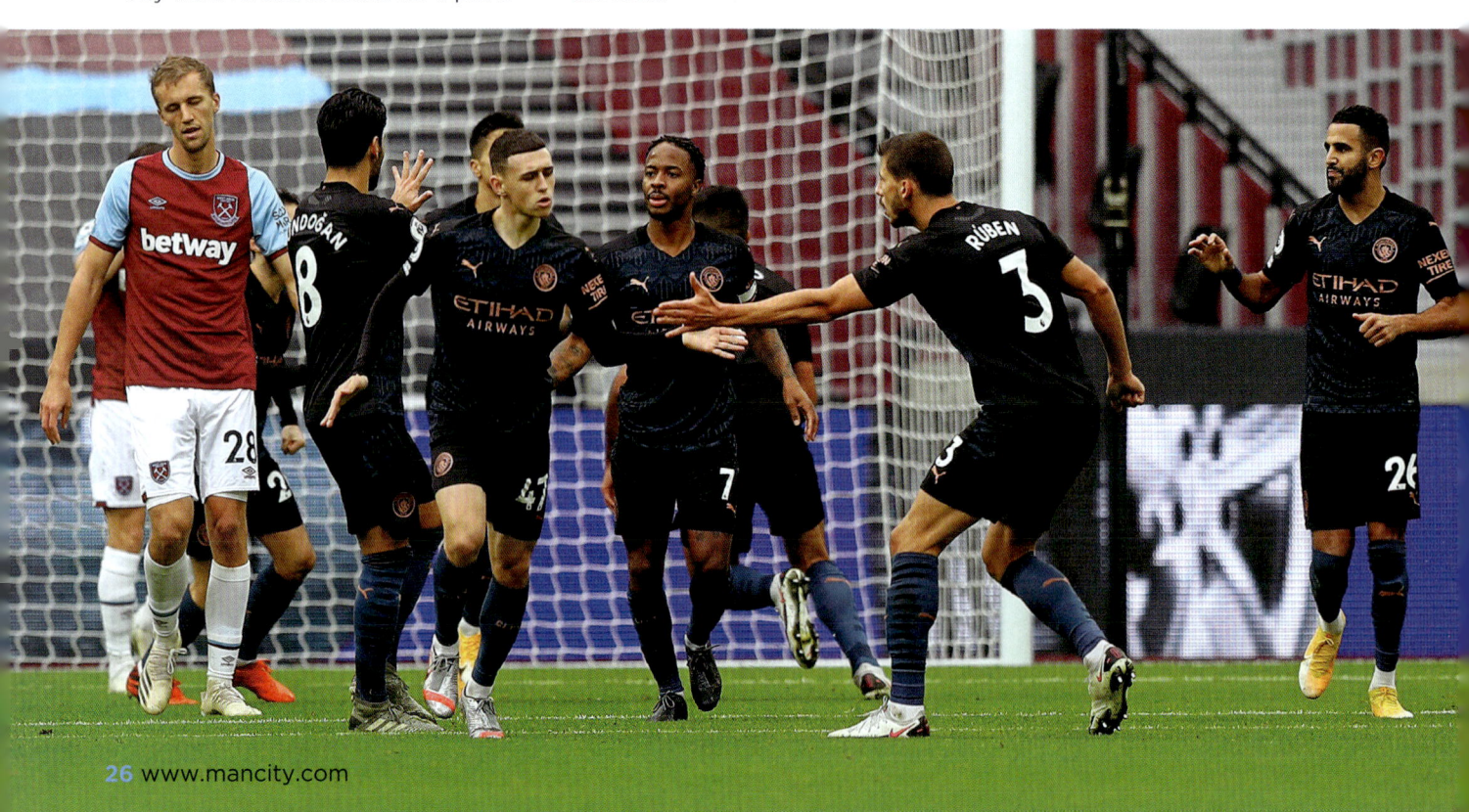

OCTOBER

# IT'S THE FOOTBALL WE PLAY – WE DON'T SIT BACK AND DEFEND, WE WANT TO SCORE MORE, WHICH IS A NIGHTMARE FOR US DEFENDERS AT TIMES!

KYLE WALKER

City then continued their fine start to this season's Champions League when they made it two wins from two in Group C by cruising to victory against Marseille.

A comfortable 3-0 win meant City made a perfect start to this season's campaign, goals from Ferran Torres, Ilkay Gundogan and Raheem Sterling sealing the three points.

Four days later Kyle Walker proved the man of the moment as he fired us to a crucial Premier League win at Sheffield United.

Making his 100th Premier League appearance for the Club, Walker rifled home a superb long-range shot against his boyhood Club to give us a first half lead.

And though the Blades sought to put us under pressure, a fine all-round display ensured that we secured a deserved victory.

## Kyle Walker marks Premier League century in style and named Etihad Player of the Month

**Making his 100th Premier League start for City, Kyle Walker scored a rare goal against Sheffield United to cap a fine month which saw him voted the Etihad Player of the Month**

Sheffield-born Walker's family still live in the city, meaning the flying right-back had to keep a lid on his celebrations to spare his parents some grief.

"My mum and dad live here, so if I'd celebrated I'd have got a lot of stick!" he said. "I'm a Sheffield United fan, too, so I couldn't celebrate."

---

21.10.20
Etihad Stadium, Champions League

**MAN CITY**     **3**
Aguero (pen 20) Gundogan (65) Torres (73)

**PORTO**     **1**
Diaz (14)

---

24.10.20
London Stadium, Premier League

**WEST HAM UNITED**     **1**
Antonio (18)

**MAN CITY**     **1**
Foden (51)

---

27.10.20
Stade Velodrome, Champions League

**MARSEILLE**     **0**

**MAN CITY**     **3**
Torres (18) Gundogan (76) Sterling (81)

---

31.10.20
Bramall Lane, Premier League

**SHEFFIELD UNITED**     **0**

**MAN CITY**     **1**
Walker (28)

www.mancity.com 27

PREMIER LEAGUE CHAMPIONS 20/21

# Olympic
## class standard

### City continue Champions League quest in style

IT was more of the same as November rolled around, Gabriel Jesus marking his return to action with a killer second goal as our perfect start to the Champions League group stage continued with a 3-0 win over Greek champions Olympiakos.

Ferran Torres scored early on before Jesus climbed off the bench to seal victory after coming on for the final 20 minutes.

Joao Cancelo then added further gloss to the scoreline with a delightful curling effort just before stoppage time to cap off a clinical and impressive performance under the Etihad lights.

It was an altogether tighter affair the following weekend as we came from behind to earn a point against Liverpool in a box office clash that didn't disappoint.

Liverpool drew first blood on 13 minutes thanks to a Mo Salah penalty before Gabriel Jesus levelled just past the half-hour.

Just before the break Kevin De Bruyne missed a penalty after Joe Gomez had handled in the box and Jesus missed a header after the break as the game ended in a 1-1 draw.

## NOVEMBER

**03.11.20**
Etihad Stadium, Champions League

**MAN CITY** 3
Torres (12) Jesus (81) Cancelo (90)

**OLYMPIAKOS** 0

**08.11.20**
Etihad Stadium, Premier League

**MAN CITY** 1
Jesus (31)

**LIVERPOOL** 1
Salah (pen 13)

www.mancity.com 29

**Together Matters** | etisalat

Etisalat is the **fastest** mobile network on Earth

Based on analysis by Ookla® of Speedtest Intelligence® data Q2-Q3 2020

# HERE FOR CITY, HERE FOR YOU.

As the Official Recruitment Partner of Manchester City, we are helping the Club build a successful team of professionals off the pitch.

And we're just as dedicated to helping you achieve your goals too.

So whatever success means to you – whether you're keen to take your career to the next level or looking to sign new talent for your organisation – Hays' devoted team of experts are here for you.

**HAYS. BEHIND EVERY GOAL.**
hays.co.uk

**HAYS** Recruiting experts worldwide
OFFICIAL RECRUITMENT PARTNER

# NOVEMBER

The international break saw Pep Guardiola sign a new deal, but momentum on the pitch couldn't be maintained as goals from Heung-Min Son and Giovani Lo Celso consigned us to a second defeat of the season.

Despite being on the front foot for much of the contest, we were unable to find a way through the home side's stubborn defence as we lost 2-0.

However, that was soon forgotten as we booked our place in the last 16 of the Champions League with a well-deserved victory in Greece, maintaining our 100% winning record in this season's competition with a 1-0 win over Olympiakos, Phil Foden scoring the winner.

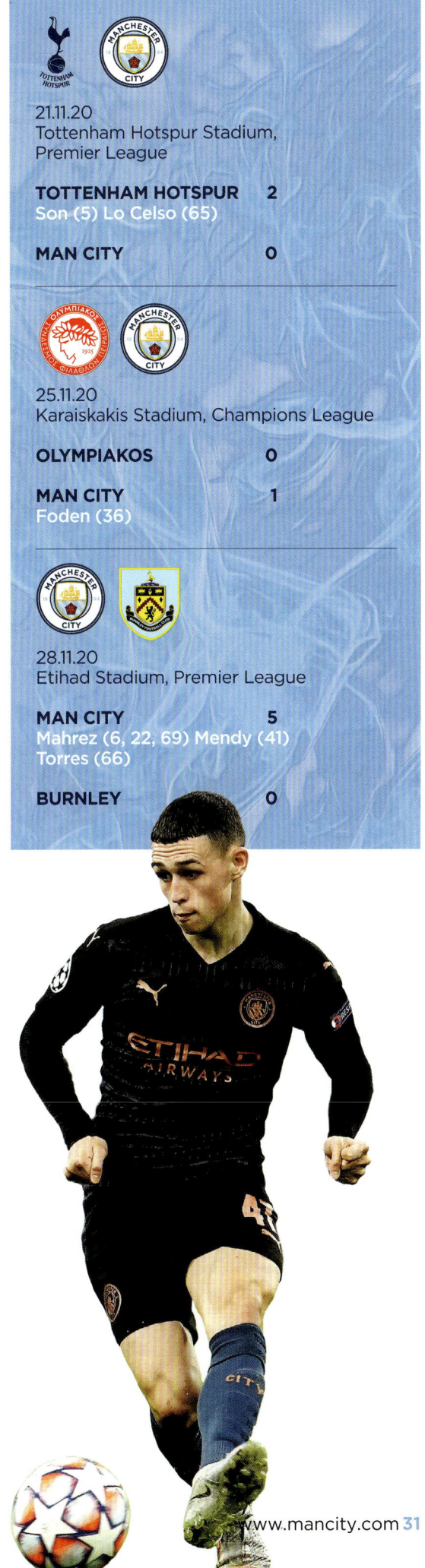

### 21.11.20
Tottenham Hotspur Stadium, Premier League

**TOTTENHAM HOTSPUR**    2
Son (5) Lo Celso (65)

**MAN CITY**    0

### 25.11.20
Karaiskakis Stadium, Champions League

**OLYMPIAKOS**    0

**MAN CITY**    1
Foden (36)

### 28.11.20
Etihad Stadium, Premier League

**MAN CITY**    5
Mahrez (6, 22, 69) Mendy (41) Torres (66)

**BURNLEY**    0

www.mancity.com 31

PREMIER LEAGUE CHAMPIONS 20/21

# Pep puts pen to paper

Pep Guardiola put pen to paper on a new two year deal this month, to keep him at the Etihad until the summer of 2023.

Speaking of his gratitude for the support he has received during his time at City, he said: "As a manager, I have everything that I need.

"Of course, all managers depend on results, obviously me as well and we have to win to continue.

"What we are right now is really, really good and the target again is fighting all together. We want to maintain this level in UK, Europe as best as possible."

### PEP GUARDIOLA
**TROPHIES WON AT CITY**

| PREMIER LEAGUE | 2017/18, 2018/19, 2020/21 |
|---|---|
| FA CUP | 2018/19 |
| LEAGUE CUP | 2017/18, 2018/19, 2019/20, 2020/21 |
| COMMUNITY SHIELD | 2018/19, 2019/20 |

**WHAT WE ARE RIGHT NOW IS REALLY, REALLY GOOD AND THE TARGET AGAIN IS FIGHTING ALL TOGETHER. WE WANT TO MAINTAIN THIS LEVEL IN UK, EUROPE AS BEST AS POSSIBLE**

www.mancity.com

NOVEMBER

And we rounded off the month in style, Riyad Mahrez hitting a first City hat-trick as Burnley were handed a fourth successive 5-0 thrashing at the Etihad.

Benjamin Mendy grabbed his first goal for the Club and Ferran Torres also got on the scoresheet as the Clarets endured yet another miserable trip to the blue half of Manchester.

## Dias voted November Player of the Month

**Ruben Dias was voted Etihad Player of the Month for November after we conceded just three goals in the whole of the month.**
John Stones narrowly missed out on the prize with Joao Cancelo also polling many votes in one of the closest player of the month contests yet.

### RUBEN DIAS PERSONAL STATS

| DATE OF BIRTH | PLACE OF BIRTH | POSITION | MAN CITY DEBUT |
|---|---|---|---|
| 14TH MAY 1997 | AMADORA, PORTUGAL | CENTRE BACK | v LEEDS UNITED PREMIER LEAGUE 03.10.20 |

www.mancity.com 33

NEXEN
NEXEN TIRE
OFFICIAL PARTNER OF
MANCHESTER CITY FOOTBALL CLUB
NEXEN
TIRE
NEXEN NEXEN TIRE

DECEMBER

# Pack leaders
## City sit top of Euro pile
Porto draw enough to confirm top spot

www.mancity.com

## PREMIER LEAGUE CHAMPIONS 20/21

**01.12.20**
Estadio do Dragao, Champions League

| PORTO | 0 |
|---|---|
| MAN CITY | 0 |

**05.12.20**
Etihad Stadium, Premier League

| MAN CITY | 2 |
|---|---|
| Sterling (5) De Bruyne (pen 26) | |
| FULHAM | 0 |

**09.12.20**
Etihad Stadium, Champions League

| MAN CITY | 3 |
|---|---|
| Torres (48) Aguero (77) Gonzalez (og 90) | |
| MARSEILLE | 0 |

**12.12.20**
Old Trafford, Premier League

| MANCHESTER UNITED | 0 |
|---|---|
| MAN CITY | 0 |

**CITY confirmed top spot in Champions League Group C after a largely bad-tempered goalless draw at a dogged Porto.**

We enjoyed the majority of the play and also had a late goal ruled out by VAR but we were ultimately unable to break down our well-oiled and regimented hosts, who also secured their place in the Last 16 with a point.

In the Premier League, Pep Guardiola celebrated his 250th match in charge of City – and his 700th game overall as a manager – as first-half goals from Raheem Sterling and Kevin De Bruyne propelled us to a comfortable 2-0 victory over Fulham at the Etihad Stadium.

36 www.mancity.com

And back in the Champions League, Sergio Aguero returned to first team action in style, scoring just 10 minutes into his long-awaited comeback as we ended the Group C schedule with a 3-0 win over Marseille.

Ferran Torres had put us ahead just after half-time and Raheem Sterling scored in added time, but it was Aguero who grabbed the headlines for his stellar cameo off the bench.

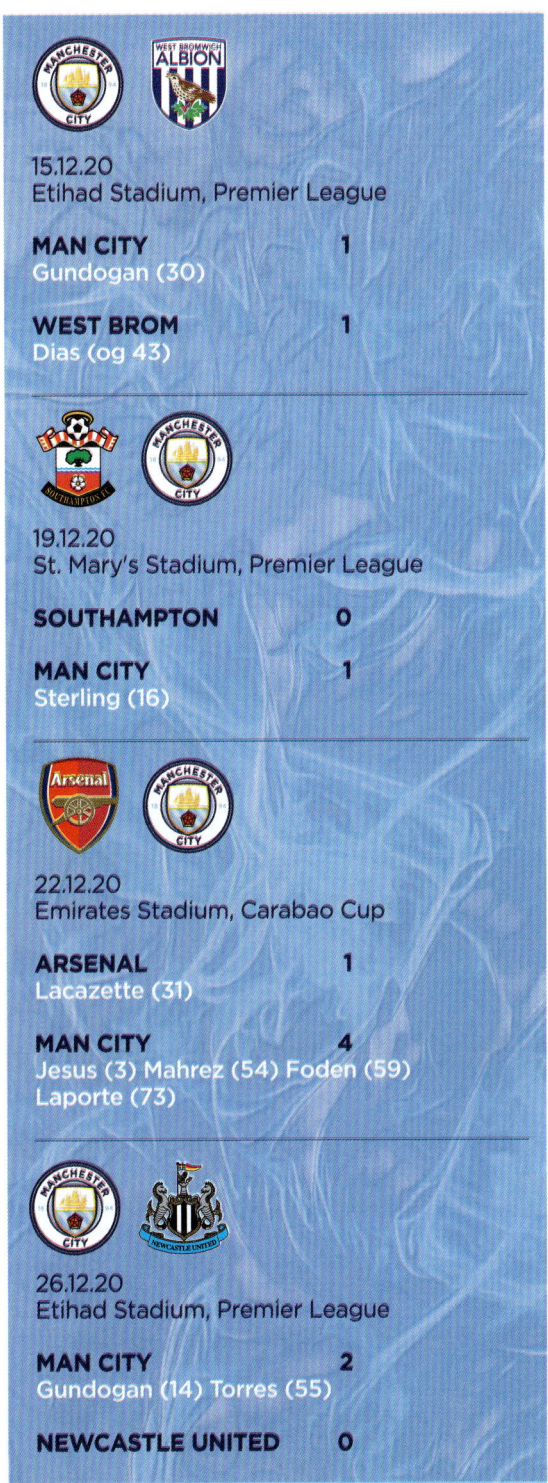

## DECEMBER

**15.12.20**
Etihad Stadium, Premier League

| MAN CITY | 1 |
|---|---|
| Gundogan (30) | |
| **WEST BROM** | **1** |
| Dias (og 43) | |

**19.12.20**
St. Mary's Stadium, Premier League

| SOUTHAMPTON | 0 |
|---|---|
| **MAN CITY** | **1** |
| Sterling (16) | |

**22.12.20**
Emirates Stadium, Carabao Cup

| ARSENAL | 1 |
|---|---|
| Lacazette (31) | |
| **MAN CITY** | **4** |
| Jesus (3) Mahrez (54) Foden (59) Laporte (73) | |

**26.12.20**
Etihad Stadium, Premier League

| MAN CITY | 2 |
|---|---|
| Gundogan (14) Torres (55) | |
| **NEWCASTLE UNITED** | **0** |

# WE ARE IN THE NEXT ROUND AND WE SEE THE TEAMS WHO HAVE QUALIFIED ARE INCREDIBLE

**PEP GUARDIOLA**

www.mancity.com

**PREMIER LEAGUE CHAMPIONS 20/21**

Three days later the 183rd Manchester derby ended with honours even as we shared the spoils with United in a goalless stalemate at Old Trafford.

United saw a penalty overturned by VAR and our best chance fell to Riyad Mahrez who saw his shot well saved by David de Gea, but chances remained at a premium as both sides eventually settled for a point apiece.

DECEMBER

And we endured a frustrating evening the following Tuesday as a committed West Bromwich Albion earned a 1-1 draw at the Etihad Stadium.

The Premier League strugglers came from a Ilkay Gundogan goal down with a fortuitous leveller just before the break and held firm after the break despite constant City pressure.

Albion keeper Sam Johnstone made two point-blank saves in added time to preserve the visitors' point.

**PREMIER LEAGUE CHAMPIONS 20/21**

It was back to winning ways against Southampton, though, as we battled to a 1-0 victory on the south coast, with Raheem Sterling netting the only goal of the game early on.

Sterling calmly converted from 12-yards after he was expertly picked out by Kevin De Bruyne's ball across goal in the 16th minute to end our two-match winless run.

Second half strikes from Riyad Mahrez, Phil Foden and Aymeric Laporte plus an early Gabriel Jesus header helped us book our place in the Carabao Cup semi-finals with a dominant 4-1 win over Arsenal.

It was another League Cup masterclass on a night to remember in North London, the victory further extending Pep Guardiola's incredible record in the competition and it was no less than we deserved after what was another impressive all-round display.

DECEMBER

And we rounded off the year brilliantly as Ilkay Gundogan and Ferran Torres scored to maintain our fine Premier League home record against Newcastle United with a comfortable 2-0 win on Boxing Day.

Gundogan fired home from six-yards early in the first half and Torres wrapped up the points after the break with a close range finish to seal our 12th consecutive league victory over the Magpies at the Etihad Stadium, to make it 10 games unbeaten in all competitions.

## IT WAS THE BEST PERFORMANCE OF THE SEASON. THE PLAYERS WERE INCREDIBLE – EVERYONE WAS SO FOCUSED AND WE MADE A GOOD PERFORMANCE

PEP GUARDIOLA

## DE BRUYNE NAMED IN FIFPRO WORLD XI

**Kevin De Bruyne capped a remarkable year when he was named in the 2020 FIFPRO World XI.**

Voted for by professional footballers across the globe, it was just the latest prestigious accolade bestowed on the midfielder and provided the perfect end to a wonderful 2020 for a player now widely recognised as one of the world's finest.

The 29-year-old was also named as the 2019-20 Premier League Playmaker, the Premier League Player of the Season, the PFA Player of the Year and the UEFA Midfielder of the Season during a spectacular calendar year.

Pep Guardiola said: "All of us here at Manchester City are happy and proud Kevin has been selected in this incredible team containing the best XI players of the year.

"His vision, speed of thought, the detailed way he sees the game and his technical quality mean he possesses everything a top midfielder needs to excel.

"We are lucky to have him at Manchester City."

www.mancity.com 41

PREMIER LEAGUE CHAMPIONS 20/21

JANUARY

# Invincible
## City unbeaten

### Foden springs to life as we stride on

**INTO the new year and City produced a blistering performance to beat Chelsea 3-1 at Stamford Bridge in our first game of 2021.**

The hard work was all done in the space of 16 first-half minutes that blew Frank Lampard's side away.

Goals from Ilkay Gundogan, Phil Foden and Kevin De Bruyne meant there was no way back for the hosts who were outplayed for the majority of the game before pulling a goal back with almost the last kick of the contest.

---

03.01.21
Stamford Bridge, Premier League

| **CHELSEA** | **1** |
|---|---|
| Callum Hudson-Odoi (90) | |

| **MAN CITY** | **3** |
|---|---|
| Gundogan (18) Foden (21) De Bruyne (34) | |

---

06.01.21
Old Trafford, Carabao Cup

| **MANCHESTER UNITED** | **0** |
|---|---|

| **MAN CITY** | **2** |
|---|---|
| Stones (50) Fernandinho (83) | |

---

10.01.21
Etihad Stadium, FA Cup Third Round

| **MAN CITY** | **3** |
|---|---|
| Silva (8, 15) Foden (33) | |

| **BIRMINGHAM CITY** | **0** |
|---|---|

www.mancity.com 43

**PREMIER LEAGUE CHAMPIONS 20/21**

City reached the Carabao Cup final for the fourth year in a row after beating Manchester United 2-0 in an entertaining Manchester derby at Old Trafford.

John Stones steered in Phil Foden's free-kick to give us the lead early in the second half and Fernandinho fired in a 20-yard volley to seal a deserved semi-final victory and our place in the final.

A minute's silence was held before kick-off in memory of Colin Bell, who passed away the day before, and City's dominant performance was a fitting tribute to a man widely regarded as one of the greatest players in the Club's history.

## COLIN BELL: 1946-2021

**It was with the deepest sadness and heaviest of hearts that we announced the passing of Manchester City legend Colin Bell on January 5.**

Colin passed away peacefully after a short illness, aged 74, leaving behind wife Marie, children Jon and Dawn and grandchildren, Luke, Mark, Isla and Jack.

He is generally considered to be the finest City player of his generation, making 501 appearances and scoring 153 goals for the Club during a 13-year stay.

Known as Colin The King, in 2004 fans voted to name a stand inside the Etihad Stadium after him and his name is still sung regularly at matches.

Few players have left such an indelible mark on City.

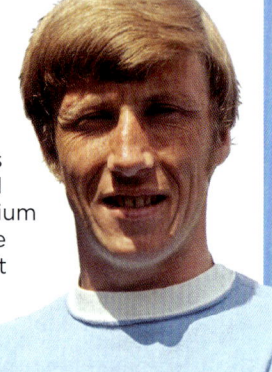

JANUARY

City moved safely into the Fourth Round of the FA Cup with an emphatic 3-0 win over Birmingham at the Etihad.

Pep Guardiola's men made light work of the Championship side, delivering a ruthless attacking display full of verve and class.

Bernardo Silva put us ahead with a brilliant left-footed volley from the edge of the area, and the Portuguese midfielder then doubled our lead, finishing off a fine team goal with a close-range strike.

Phil Foden soon made it 3-0 with a powerful low strike to effectively make it game over by the half-time break.

The youngster was on target again three days later as we returned to Premier League action with a 1-0 win over Brighton & Hove Albion at the Etihad.

Bernardo struck the woodwork and Raheem Sterling missed an added time penalty, with the visitors belying their lowly position in the Premier League, but Foden's strike meant we ended the night in the top four, four points behind leaders Manchester United with a game in hand.

---

13.01.21
Etihad Stadium, Premier League

**MAN CITY**     **1**
Foden (44)

**BRIGHTON
& HOVE ALBION**     **0**

---

17.01.21
Etihad Stadium, Premier League

**MAN CITY**     **4**
Stones (26, 68) Gundogan (56)
Sterling (88)

**CRYSTAL PALACE**     **0**

---

20.01.21
Etihad Stadium, Premier League

**MAN CITY**     **2**
Silva (79) Gundogan (pen 90)

**ASTON VILLA**     **0**

www.mancity.com 45

# #WORLDCLASS PRODUCTS

## PUTTING OUR BEST LINEUP FORWARD

MANCHESTER CITY | Midea
OFFICIAL PARTNER

- BreezeleSS Air Conditioner
- Bladeless Air Purifier
- 360° Fan
- Lunar Dial Washing Machine
- Anti-Bacteria Water Heater
- Steaming Built-in Oven
- Smart Temperature Refrigerator
- Commercial Air Conditioner
- Fast + Quiet Dishwasher
- Air Fryer + Pressure Cooker
- All Terrain Robot Vacuum Cleaner

JANUARY

John Stones then scored twice as we eased to a 4-0 victory over Crystal Palace to move up the table again.

Stones netted either side of Ilkay Gundogan's brilliant 20-yard effort, before Raheem Sterling's free-kick completed the rout to extend our unbeaten run to 15 games and move us two points behind United.

A late stunner from Bernardo Silva, his first Premier League goal of the season, and an Ilkay Gundogan penalty were enough to earn City a hard fought 2-0 win against Aston Villa and move us top of the table.

City scored twice in the final 11-minutes to claim the three points which saw us leapfrog Leicester City and Manchester United, though the latter reclaimed top spot with their victory over Fulham later in the evening.

23.01.21
Johnny-Rocks Stadium, FA Cup Fourth Round

**CHELTENHAM TOWN**    1
May (59)

**MAN CITY**    3
Foden (81) Jesus (84)
Torres (90)

26.01.21
The Hawthorns, Premier League

**WEST BROM**    0

**MAN CITY**    5
Gundogan (6, 30) Cancelo (20)
Mahrez (45) Sterling (57)

30.01.21
Etihad Stadium, Premier League

**MAN CITY**    1
Jesus (9)

**SHEFFIELD UNITED**    0

www.mancity.com 47

PREMIER LEAGUE CHAMPIONS 20/21

## Phil Foden reaches 100 appearances for Man City

Phil Foden chalked up a personal milestone in his Manchester City career after making his 100th appearance for the Club.

The 20-year-old reached his century when he started in City's brilliant 5-0 win over West Bromwich Albion.

It is just the latest landmark in Foden's stellar fledgling career and arrived a little over three years after he made his first team debut as a substitute for Yaya Toure in the 1-0 Champions League win over Feyenoord in November 2017.

It wasn't so straightforward in the FA Cup the following weekend, though, as we needed three goals in the last 10 minutes to see off an excellent Cheltenham Town.

The League Two side, 72 places below City in the football pyramid, looked set to pull off one of the biggest modern-day FA Cup shocks after taking a second-half lead.

But City, prompted by the inspirational Phil Foden, scored three times in the last ten minutes through Foden, Gabriel Jesus and Ferran Torres to navigate the trickiest of ties at the Jonny-Rocks Stadium.

### ✚ PHIL FODEN PERSONAL STATS

| DATE OF BIRTH | PLACE OF BIRTH | POSITION | MAN CITY DEBUT |
|---|---|---|---|
| 28TH MAY 2000 | MANCHESTER | MIDFIELDER | v FEYENOORD CHAMPIONS LEAGUE 24.1.17 |

> **THE MOST IMPORTANT THING TO ME, RATHER THAN THE SIX VICTORIES IN A ROW, IS WE ARE BACK PLAYING THE WAY WE NEED TO PLAY TO BE CHAMPIONS. I WAS REALLY IMPRESSED WITH OUR PERFORMANCE. WE PLAYED REALLY WELL**
>
> **PEP GUARDIOLA**

JANUARY

**Gundogan voted Player of the Month for January**

**Ilkay Gundogan was voted Etihad Player of the Month for January after taking more than 70% of the Cityzens vote, beating team-mates John Stones and Joao Cancelo to the prize.**

Arguably in the form of his life, Gundogan – who was also named the Player of the Month by the Premier League – grabbed five goals during a month where his performances were nothing short of exceptional.

He also added several assists during a month City won all nine fixtures.

The scare was soon forgotten back in the Premier League, though, as we moved to the top of the table with a superb 5-0 victory away at West Brom.

A first-half blitz, inspired by the excellent Ilkay Gundogan, saw City go into the break 4-0 up.

Gundogan (2), Joao Cancelo and Riyad Mahrez ended the game as a contest before half-time, with Raheem Sterling bagging a fifth before an hour had been played.

And City made it 12 straight wins in all competitions with a 1-0 victory over Sheffield United at the Etihad as Pep Guardiola made it 500 wins as a manager.

Gabriel Jesus scored the winner inside 10 minutes, finishing from close range after fine work from Ferran Torres who went past Jayden Bogle and Ethan Ampadu inside the area before squaring for the Brazilian.

By no means our most compelling performance, the win made it 19 games unbeaten in all competitions, our last defeat coming away at Tottenham in November.

And winning all nine games we played in January set a record as the most games won by a team in the top four tiers of English football in a single month since the formation of the Football League in 1888.

www.mancity.com 49

PREMIER LEAGUE CHAMPIONS 20/21

# City hit four
## against Liverpool

Gundogan in the goals to extend lead at top

FEBRUARY

03.02.21
Turf Moor, Premier League

**BURNLEY** 0

**MAN CITY** 2
Jesus (3) Sterling (38)

07.02.21
Anfield, Premier League

**LIVERPOOL** 1
Salah (pen 63)

**MAN CITY** 4
Gundogan (49, 73) Sterling (76)
Foden (83)

10.02.21
Liberty Stadium, FA Cup Fifth Round

**SWANSEA CITY** 1
Whittaker (77)

**MAN CITY** 3
Walker (30) Sterling (47) Jesus (50)

**PREMIER LEAGUE CHAMPIONS 20/21**

**WE extended our lead at the top of the Premier League thanks to a dominant 13th consecutive victory in all competitions away at Burnley.**

First-half strikes from Gabriel Jesus and skipper Raheem Sterling sent Pep Guardiola's side in at the break 2-0 ahead at Turf Moor.

And that's how the score remained as we moved three points clear of second-placed Manchester United.

We then ended decades of hurt at Anfield by soundly beating Liverpool 4-1 on a memorable afternoon on Merseyside.

Phil Foden scored one and assisted another as a rampant City recorded our first victory at the stadium since 2003.

City missed a first-half penalty before two Ilkay Gundogan goals – with a Mo Salah penalty sandwiched in-between – and further goals from Raheem Sterling and the irrepressible Foden completed the rout.

That made it 14 wins on the bounce and 21 games unbeaten - and for once, it was a very happy trip home from Anfield.

FEBRUARY

13.02.21
Etihad Stadium, Premier League

**MAN CITY**     **3**
Rodri (pen 23) Gundogan (50, 66)

**TOTTENHAM HOTSPUR**     **0**

17.02.21
Goodison Park, Premier League

**EVERTON**     **1**
Richarlison (37)

**MAN CITY**     **3**
Foden (32) Mahrez (63) Silva (77)

City made it through to the FA Cup quarter-finals after beating promotion-chasing Championship side Swansea City at The Liberty Stadium.

Kyle Walker opened the scoring in the first-half, with two quickfire goals after the break from Raheem Sterling and Gabriel Jesus sending us on our way to a 3-1 win.

Back in league action, Ilkay Gundogan's sensational goalscoring form continued as we comfortably beat Tottenham Hotspur.

The German scored for the second league game in succession after Rodrigo's penalty had given us a 23rd minute lead in what was a deserved victory against the last team to beat us.

## Guardiola clocks up double century of City wins

**Our 3-1 win over Swansea in the FA Cup Fifth Round was Pep Guardiola's 200th as City manager.**

The boss took charge in the summer of 2016 and has had a transformational effect on the Club's playing style, guiding us to nine major trophies so far.

The Swansea win made it a remarkable 659 goals in 268 matches – an average of 2.46 per game.

Guardiola was also named Premier League Manager of the Month for the second consecutive month after our 100% record earned him the February prize.

The Catalan picked up January's award after a perfect six game streak and repeated the trick this month when he again led City to six victories in as many matches.

Burnley, Everton, Arsenal and West Ham United were all beaten, though the highlight of this brilliant run came when Guardiola masterminded convincing back-to-back victories over Liverpool and Tottenham Hotspur.

www.mancity.com 53

# axi

## Experience a trading partner **who's behind you all the way.**

**TRADE YOUR EDGE**

Forex | Commodities | Indices | Gold

**77% of retail investor accounts lose money when trading CFDs with this provider.**
You should consider whether you understand how CFDs work and whether you can afford to take the high risk of losing your money.

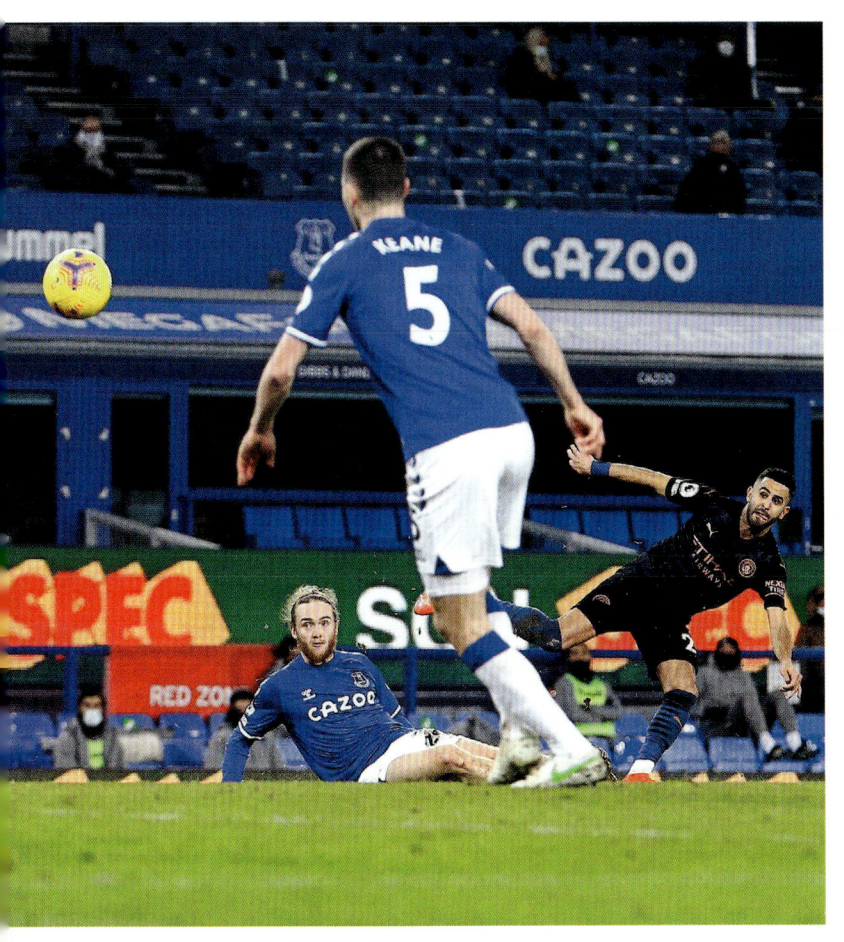

FEBRUARY

And we then extended our lead at the top of the Premier League table to 10 points with an impressive 3-1 win over Everton at Goodison Park.

Goals from Phil Foden, Riyad Mahrez and Bernardo Silva sealed the victory, with Pep Guardiola's side becoming the first English side to record 10 consecutive top-flight league wins at the start of a year.

21.02.21
Emirates Stadium, Premier League

| **ARSENAL** | **0** |
|---|---|
| **MAN CITY** | **1** |

Sterling (2)

24.02.21
Puskas Arena, Champions League

| **BORUSSIA MONCHENGLADBACH** | **0** |
|---|---|
| **MAN CITY** | **2** |

Silva (29) Jesus (65)

27.02.21
Etihad Stadium, Premier League

| **MAN CITY** | **2** |
|---|---|
| **WEST HAM UNITED** | **1** |

Dias (30) Stones (68)
Antonio (43)

www.mancity.com 55

**PREMIER LEAGUE CHAMPIONS 20/21**

On to Arsenal at the Emirates, and we made it 18 straight wins in all competitions – and equalled our club record 11 consecutive away victories – by beating the Gunners 1-0.

Raheem Sterling headed home from Riyad Mahrez's inch-perfect cross to give us a dream start inside two minutes and that turned out to be the winner, with our play thereafter rarely hitting the heights of recent weeks due to Arsenal's diligence and squeezing of space.

The records kept falling as goals from Bernardo Silva and Gabriel Jesus helped to secure a superb Champions League last 16 first leg triumph over Borussia Monchengladbach.

Pep Guardiola's side were in imperious form once again at the Puskas Arena in Budapest as we racked up a 19th consecutive win – and created English history for a top-flight team by chalking up a 12th straight away victory.

56 www.mancity.com

FEBRUARY

**TO HAVE 20 WINS IN THIS PERIOD, I THINK THIS COULD BE THE GREATEST ACHIEVEMENT WE HAVE DONE. IT DOESN'T MEAN WE HAVE WON THE TITLE OF COURSE, BUT IN WINTER TIME IN ENGLAND, EVERY THREE DAYS A GAME, COVID-19 SITUATION, INJURIES... WINNING, WINNING, WINNING SHOWS STRENGTH, MENTALITY. NO COMPLAINTS. WE CREATED A LOT, THAT'S WHY IT'S GOOD** PEP GUARDIOLA

Back in the Premier League, we had to work hard to see off a stubborn and determined West Ham at the Etihad.

Goals from Ruben Dias and John Stones either side of an Antonio equaliser gave us a 2-1 win – our 20th on the bounce – to extend our lead at the top of the table to 13 points.

### MAHREZ VOTED PLAYER OF THE MONTH

**Riyad Mahrez was voted City's Etihad Player of the Month for February.**

The Algerian winger was in sizzling form and his efforts were rewarded when he took a huge 79% of the poll on our Cityzens platform, from nearly 30,000 votes registered.

Bernardo finished second and Rodrigo third.

Ilkay Gündogan, meanwhile, was named the Premier League's Player of the Month for the second month in a row.

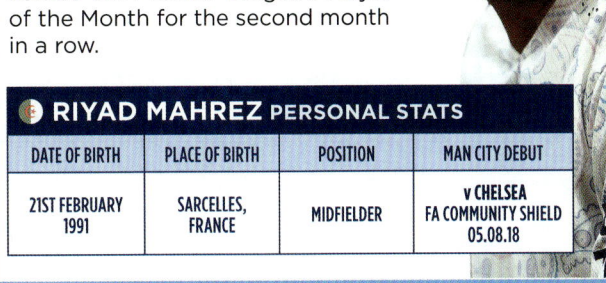

PLAYER OF THE MONTH
26
RIYAD MAHREZ

#### RIYAD MAHREZ PERSONAL STATS

| DATE OF BIRTH | PLACE OF BIRTH | POSITION | MAN CITY DEBUT |
|---|---|---|---|
| 21ST FEBRUARY 1991 | SARCELLES, FRANCE | MIDFIELDER | v CHELSEA FA COMMUNITY SHIELD 05.08.18 |

www.mancity.com 57

# PREMIER LEAGUE CHAMPIONS 2020/21

## GAME CHANGER

footballfoundation.org.uk

MARCH

# Marching on
## as records start to tumble
Jesus brace gets month off to a flyer

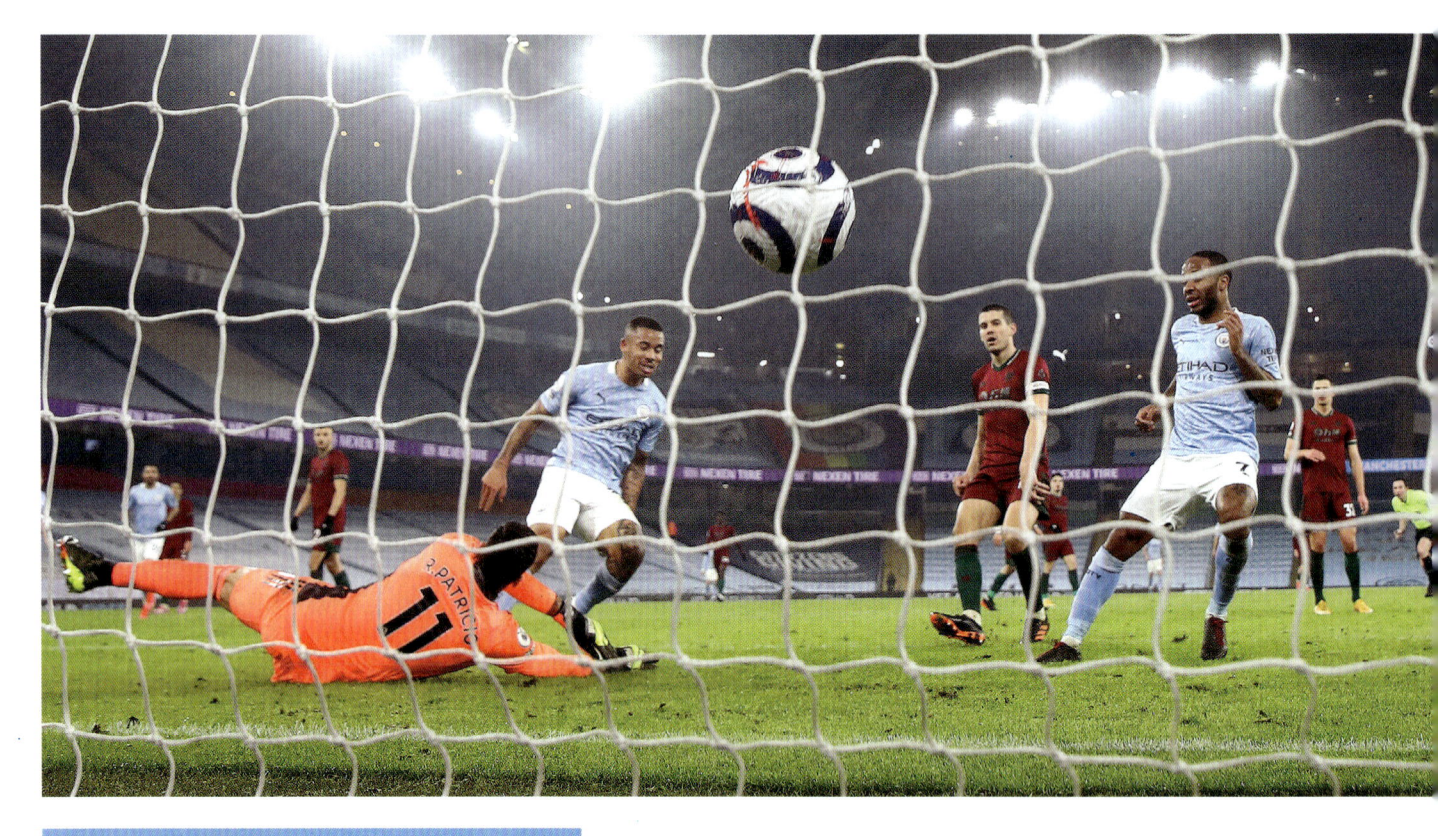

**PREMIER LEAGUE CHAMPIONS 20/21**

02.03.21
Etihad Stadium, Premier League

| MAN CITY | 4 |
|---|---|
Dendoncker (og 15) Jesus (80, 90) Mahrez (90)

| WOLVES | 1 |
|---|---|
Coady (61)

07.03.21
Etihad Stadium, Premier League

| MAN CITY | 0 |
|---|---|

| MANCHESTER UNITED | 2 |
|---|---|
Fernandes (pen 2) Shaw (50)

10.03.21
Etihad Stadium, Premier League

| MAN CITY | 5 |
|---|---|
De Bruyne (15, 59) Mahrez (40, 55) Gundogan (45)

| SOUTHAMPTON | 2 |
|---|---|
Ward-Prowse (pen 25) Adams (56)

**OUR unbeaten run stretched to a Club record-equalling 28 games as we eased to a comfortable 4-1 victory over Wolverhampton Wanderers to consolidate our position at the top of the Premier League.**

City were in control from the first whistle and took the lead when Leander Dendoncker turned Riyad Mahrez's cross into his own net in the 15th minute, but Conor Coady netted a surprise equaliser when he headed in from Joao Moutinho's free-kick just past the hour mark.

Our response was emphatic, however, as three goals in the final 10 minutes, from Gabriel Jesus (2) and Mahrez, helped us seal a 21st consecutive win in all competitions.

That proud winning run and long unbeaten stretch came to a disappointing end the following weekend, though, as we succumbed to a 2-0 defeat at home to Manchester United.

City were caught cold after conceding a first minute penalty, scored by Bruno Fernandes, and we never really recovered, going further behind just after the restart to a Luke Shaw goal.

60 www.mancity.com

MARCH

13.03.21
Craven Cottage, Premier League

**FULHAM** 0

**MAN CITY** 3
Stones (47) Jesus (56) Aguero (pen 60)

16.03.21
Puskas Arena, Champions League

**MAN CITY** 2
De Bruyne (12) Gundogan (18)

**BORUSSIA MONCHENGLADBACH** 0

MAN CITY WIN 4 - 0 ON AGGREGATE

20.03.21
Goodison Park, FA Cup, Quarter-Final

**EVERTON** 0

**MAN CITY** 2
Gundogan (84) De Bruyne (90)

But we bounced back in style with a thrilling 5-2 win over Southampton as braces from Riyad Mahrez and Kevin De Bruyne plus another Ilkay Gundogan goal helped us grab all three points.

Saints came to play football and played their part in an entertaining match, but the victory ultimately restored our 14-point lead at the top of the table with nine games remaining.

www.mancity.com 61

**PREMIER LEAGUE CHAMPIONS 20/21**

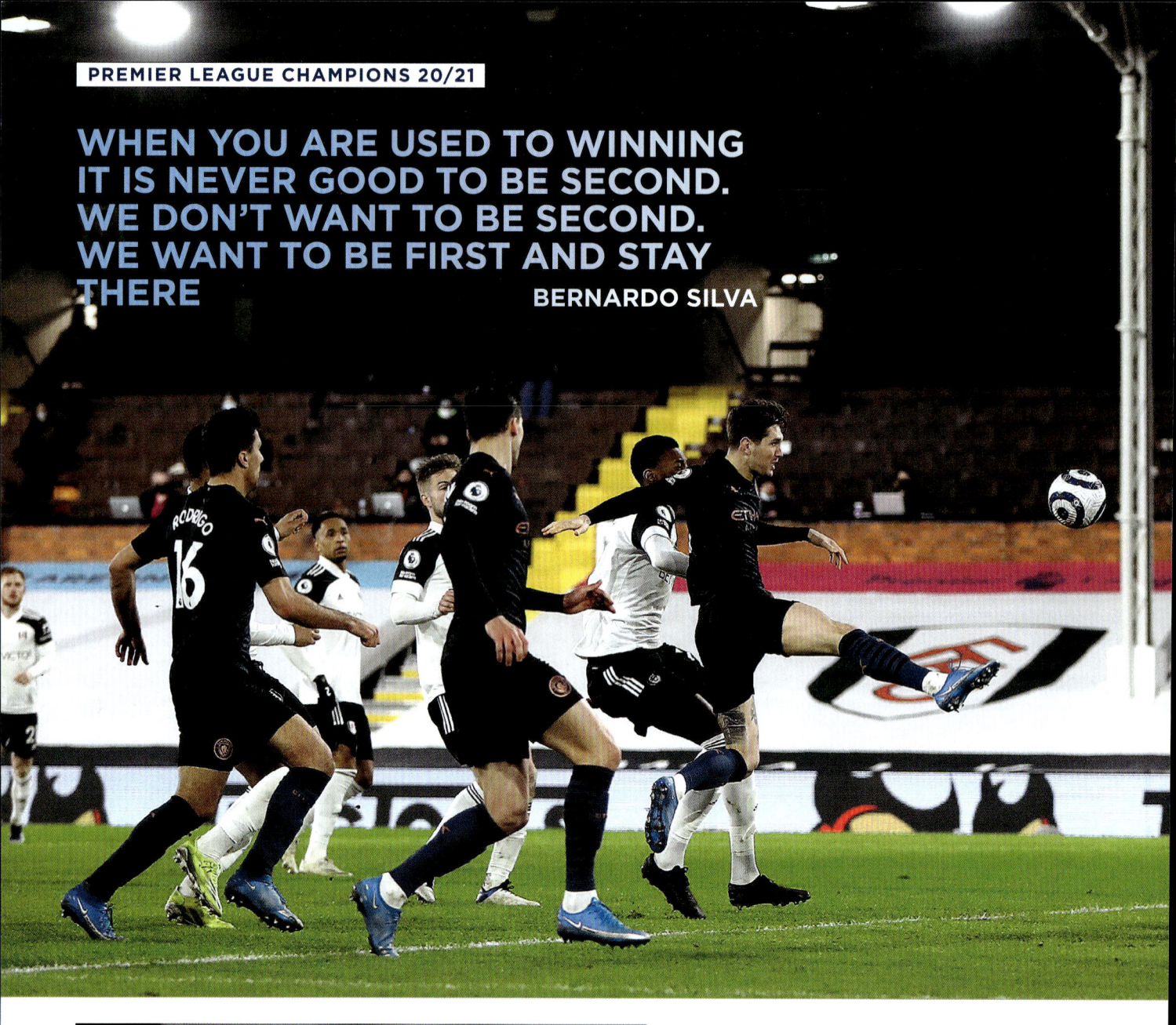

# WHEN YOU ARE USED TO WINNING IT IS NEVER GOOD TO BE SECOND. WE DON'T WANT TO BE SECOND. WE WANT TO BE FIRST AND STAY THERE
**BERNARDO SILVA**

Next up, we produced a fine second-half performance to beat Fulham 3-0 and extend our unbeaten run away from home to a club record-equalling 16 matches.

John Stones, Gabriel Jesus and a Sergio Aguero penalty did the damage, with three goals in 15 minutes securing a crucial three points in our bid to regain the Premier League title.

Aguero's was his first Premier League goal in 417 days – a wonderful sight for City fans everywhere after his injury-affected year.

62 www.mancity.com

MARCH

Back in the Champions League, a Kevin De Bruyne stunner and clinical Ilkay Gundogan finish inside 20 minutes were enough to hand us a 2-0 Champions League last-16 second-leg victory over Borussia Monchengladbach.

Some of the football was a delight to watch, with City very much looking like a team on a mission and the only surprise was there was no further scoring in what was a sparkling display that smacked of hunger and steely determination from every player in sky blue.

## TO DO WHAT WE HAVE DONE - WINNING AND WINNING - IS BECAUSE THESE GUYS HAVE SOMETHING SPECIAL

**PEP GUARDIOLA**

www.mancity.com 63

**PREMIER LEAGUE CHAMPIONS 20/21**

Rounding off the month, City booked a place in the semi-final of the FA Cup for the third succesive season, thanks to a hard-fought 2-0 win over Everton at Goodison Park.

It was a dominant display throughout the tie from City, but a resilient Everton defence meant the two sides went in at half time all-square.

City's pressure finally paid off five minutes from time, however, as an Aymeric Laporte strike crashed off the bar and into the path of Ilkay Gundogan, who headed home the all-important opener from 10 yards.

Kevin De Bruyne then broke through to score our second goal of the tie in the final moments to book a place in the semi-final at Wembley in April.

64 www.mancity.com

MARCH

## GUARDIOLA HAILS 'REMARKABLE' FOUR MONTHS

**Pep Guardiola described City's record since the November defeat to Tottenham as "remarkable".**

City's 2-0 win away at Everton in the FA Cup at the end of March was their 33rd game in all competitions since the Tottenham set-back, a run of games which saw them win 29, draw three and lose just once.

And Guardiola hailed his side's wonderful consistency during the winter months as one of the greatest achievements during his City tenure.

"We have to adapt - every game is different," he said. "But when you win a lot of games like we have in the last four months, it's because you can adapt. That pleases me the most.

"It's not just tactics, it's mental - being ready every game.

"What we have done is more than remarkable. It's incredible. One of the greatest achievements we have done together.

"In this winter time, playing every three days, with incredible commitment in every competition, I don't have any words to express that."

## DE BRUYNE WINS ETIHAD PLAYER OF THE MONTH

**Fans voted Kevin De Bruyne the Etihad Player of the Month for March.**

The Belgian midfielder beat Fernandinho and Aymeric Laporte to the prize after an impressive run of performances which saw him score four goals in five games.

It was a typically influential period for De Bruyne, who showed signs of his best form as we approached the business end of the season.

He scored twice in the convincing 5-2 win over Southampton and followed that up with a sensational 20-yard effort that broke the deadlock in the second leg of our Champions League last 16 victory over Borussia Monchengladbach.

And, in the FA Cup quarter-final against Everton, it was De Bruyne's impact off the bench which swung the tie in City's favour, with the 29-year-old sealing our progress to the last four with a smart run and shot late in the game.

**PS4** — PlayStation

**PLAY ONLINE WITH PLAYSTATION PLUS**

WIN AS ONE

EA SPORTS

FIFA 21

FIFA OFFICIAL LICENSED PRODUCT

© 2020 Electronic Arts Inc. EA, EA SPORTS, and the EA SPORTS logo are trademarks of Electronic Arts Inc. Official FIFA licensed product. © FIFA and FIFA's Official Licensed Product Logo are copyrights and/or trademarks of FIFA. All rights reserved. Manufactured under license by Electronic Arts Inc. All other trademarks are the property of their respective owners.

CONDITIONS AND RESTRICTIONS APPLY. SEE www.ea.com/games/fifa/fifa-21-game-and-offer-disclaimers FOR DETAILS.

Lead Partner

3
www.pegi.info

APRIL

# From the heart
## Leicester are out-foxed
Mendy gets in on the action as City close in on prize

www.mancity.com

## PREMIER LEAGUE CHAMPIONS 20/21

03.04.21
King Power Stadium, Premier League

| LEICESTER CITY | 0 |
|---|---|
| **MAN CITY** | **2** |

Mendy (58) Jesus (74)

---

06.04.21
Etihad Stadium, Champions League

| **MAN CITY** | **2** |
|---|---|

De Bruyne (19) Foden (90)

| BORUSSIA DORTMUND | 1 |
|---|---|

Reus (84)

---

10.04.21
Etihad Stadium, Premier League

| **MAN CITY** | **1** |
|---|---|

Torres (76)

| LEEDS UNITED | 2 |
|---|---|

Dallas (42, 90)

**CITY moved to within 11 points of a third Premier League title in four years with a flawless 2-0 win over high-flying Leicester.**

Dominating from start to finish, Pep Guardiola's side went 17 points clear of second-place Manchester United with goals from Benjamin Mendy and Gabriel Jesus the reward for a commanding display at the King Power Stadium.

The result meant four more wins from our remaining seven Premier League games and City would be crowned champions.

In the Champions League, Phil Foden's last-minute winner against Borussia Dortmund gave us a slender 2-1 lead to take into the quarter-final second leg.

Kevin De Bruyne had given us a first-half lead against an enterprising Dortmund side, but a failure to convert a couple of very good opportunities eventually proved costly as Marco Reus levelled five minutes from time.

But the excellent Foden had the final say, as De Bruyne's peach of a cross into the box was cushioned into the youngster's path by Ilkay Gundogan and the England star made no mistake with an angled low shot.

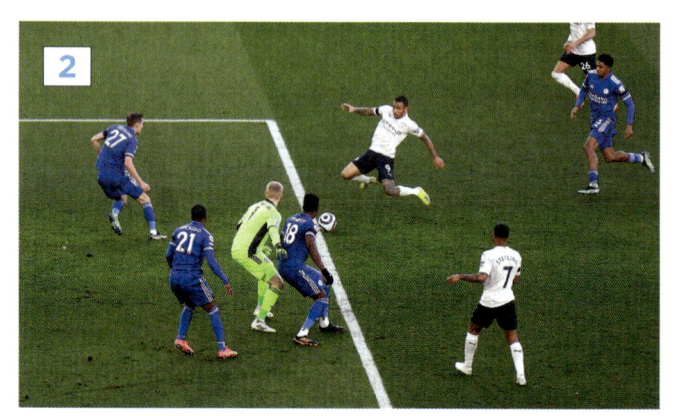

APRIL

Back in the Premier League, and City lost for only the fourth time this season as Stuart Dallas' stoppage time winner ensured 10-man Leeds United stunned the Premier League leaders at the Etihad.

Dallas gave Marcelo Bielsa's side the lead against the run of play when he fired a low 18-yard drive in off the post shortly before half-time, but Ferran Torres looked to have rescued a point when he steered Bernardo Silva's pass into the bottom corner in the 76th minute.

However, as we poured forward in search of a winner, we were undone by a slick counter-attack when Dallas latched onto Ezgjan Alioski's through ball to seal a smash and grab victory in the 91st minute.

www.mancity.com 69

**PREMIER LEAGUE CHAMPIONS 20/21**

There wasn't time to feel sorry for ourselves, though, as we came from behind four days later against Borussia Dortmund in the Champions League with a stunning second-half display to end our quarter-final jinx in style.

Trailing to an early Jude Bellingham strike, second-half goals from Riyad Mahrez and Phil Foden secured a fully deserved 2-1 victory as we moved into the last four of the competition – and a date with Paris Saint-Germain – for only the second time in our history.

Back in England and there was disappointment in our first visit to Wembley this month as our bid to win four trophies ended after a 1-0 defeat to Chelsea in the FA Cup semi-final.

# APRIL

**14.04.21**
Signal Iduna Park, Champions League

| **BORUSSIA DORTMUND** | **1** |
|---|---|
| Bellingham (15) | |

| **MAN CITY** | **2** |
|---|---|
| Mahrez (pen 55) Foden (75) | |

**MAN CITY WIN 4 - 2 ON AGGREGATE**

---

**17.04.21**
Wembley,
FA Cup, Semi Final

| **CHELSEA** | **1** |
|---|---|
| Ziyech (55) | |

| **MAN CITY** | **0** |

---

**21.04.21**
Villa Park, Premier League

| **ASTON VILLA** | **1** |
|---|---|
| McGinn (1) | |

| **MAN CITY** | **2** |
|---|---|
| Foden (22), Rodrigo (40) | |

---

**25.04.21**
Wembley, EFL Cup Final

| **MAN CITY** | **1** |
|---|---|
| Laporte (82) | |

| **TOTTENHAM HOTSPUR** | **0** |

---

**28.04.21**
Parc des Princes,
Champions League Semi-Final first leg

| **PARIS SAINT-GERMAIN** | **1** |
|---|---|
| Marquinhos (15) | |

| **MAN CITY** | **2** |
|---|---|
| De Bruyne (64) Mahrez (71) | |

---

City, who made eight changes from the side that beat Dortmund, failed to break down a resolute Chelsea defence and created only a few decent chances in what was an off-colour performance at the national stadium, as Hakim Ziyech grabbed the winner for the Londoners on 55 minutes.

In the Premier League 10-man City took another big step towards regaining the title as we stretched our lead at the top to 11 points thanks to a dramatic victory at Aston Villa.

Having fallen behind to a goal on 20 seconds from John McGinn, we hit back to lead through first half goals from Phil Foden and Rodrigo.

However, we were then reduced to 10 men on the stroke of half-time when John Stones were shown a straight red card after a challenge on Jacob Ramsey.

But, on a night of high drama in the Midlands, Villa also went a man down early after the restart as Matty Cash was shown a red card for a foul on Foden, and an impressive City held firm to secure a deserved victory.

## DE BRUYNE EXTENDS CITY CONTRACT UNTIL 2025

**Kevin De Bruyne signed a two-year extension to his current contract, keeping him at City until the summer of 2025.**

The Belgian has spent five-and-a-half years at the Etihad, a period which has seen him establish himself as one of the world's finest creative players.

It's also been an era of sustained success, with De Bruyne winning two Premier League titles, one FA Cup and four League Cups, as well as the 2020 PFA Player of the Year award.

"I could not be happier," De Bruyne said.

"This football club is geared for success. It offers me everything I need to maximise my performance, so signing this contract was a straightforward decision. I am playing the best football of my career and I honestly feel there is more to come.

"My focus now is on ensuring we have a successful end to the current campaign. Our results and performances so far have been excellent, but we need to make sure we end the season with the silverware we deserve."

www.mancity.com 71

PREMIER LEAGUE CHAMPIONS 20/21

# City Carabao Cup Kings

And then it was back to Wembley, where we won the Carabao Cup for a record-equalling eighth time after beating Tottenham Hotspur 1-0 to lift the trophy for the fourth consecutive year.

Aymeric Laporte was City's hero, heading home from Kevin De Bruyne's free-kick in the 82nd minute to give us a thoroughly deserved victory, which saw us move level with Liverpool as the most successful side in the competition's history.

With 8,000 supporters in attendance – the most at any game in England since the start of the COVID-19 pandemic – Guardiola's men rose to the occasion and the win was made all the sweeter by the sight of 2,000 City fans celebrating at full-time.

APRIL

www.mancity.com 73

PREMIER LEAGUE CHAMPIONS 20/21

**I'M REALLY HAPPY FOR MYSELF, FOR MY TEAMMATES FOR EVERYONE ASSOCIATED WITH THE CLUB. I'M REALLY PROUD TO WIN SIX TROPHIES IN THIS COMPETITION. I'M GRATEFUL FOR THIS CLUB. I'M SO HAPPY TO SEE THE FANS BACK IN THE STADIUM**

### FERNANDINHO: I'M PROUD TO CAPTAIN CITY

**Fernandinho spoke of his enormous pride and pleasure at being City captain as the squad geared up for the end of the season.**

Appointed to the position last summer after the departure of David Silva, the Brazilian midfielder says being captain has offered him a key platform from which to help and mentor his colleagues.

And the 36-year-old revealed that in taking the role, he sought valuable advice and inspiration from City's former skippers to prepare him for the crucial position.

"It's a real honour to be captain of this club, from the moment I was asked it has been a pleasure," Fernandinho declared.

"It was a special moment for me and it's something I am really enjoying.

"I've been here for eight seasons now and I spent a lot of time with the club's former captains, who I spoke to about the role within the squad.

"It's a role I am proud to have, I am involved in a lot off the pitch, I get to talk to a lot of people, it's my job to help fix things if they're not going right and that's something I have enjoyed.

"The best way to enjoy something is to always do your best when you are doing it and to help others to also do their best."

APRIL

Returning to the Champions League at the end of the month, second half goals from Kevin De Bruyne and Riyad Mahrez saw us fight back from behind to clinch a superb semi-final first leg triumph at Paris Saint-Germain.

Trailing at the break to a first-half Marquinhos header, Pep Guardiola's side staged a stunning turnaround after the break at the Parc des Princes.

Having first drawn level through skipper De Bruyne's 64th minute cross-shot, we then took an all-important lead thanks to Mahrez's 71st minute free-kick and deservedly held firm to seal a famous and crucial 2-1 victory – one of the finest in our European history – to take into the second leg.

**THIS CLUB DON'T HAVE MUCH EXPERIENCE IN THE SEMI-FINALS OF THIS TOURNAMENT. THIS WILL HELP US. IN THE SECOND HALF WE WERE AGGRESSIVE AND PLAYED REALLY GOOD**

PEP GUARDIOLA

www.mancity.com 75

**PREMIER LEAGUE CHAMPIONS 20/21**

01.05.21
Selhurst Park, Premier League

**CRYSTAL PALACE** 0

**MAN CITY** 2
Aguero (57) Torres (59)

04.05.21
Etihad Stadium, Champions League
Semi-Final second Leg

**MAN CITY** 2
Mahrez (11, 63)

**PARIS SAINT-GERMAIN** 0

Man City win 4-1 on aggregate

08.05.21
Etihad Stadium, Premier League

**MAN CITY** 1
Sterling (44)

**CHELSEA** 2
Ziyech (63) Alonso (90)

76 www.mancity.com

MAY

# Final flourish
## sees City fight to the end
### Champions League beckons as Premier League title is secured

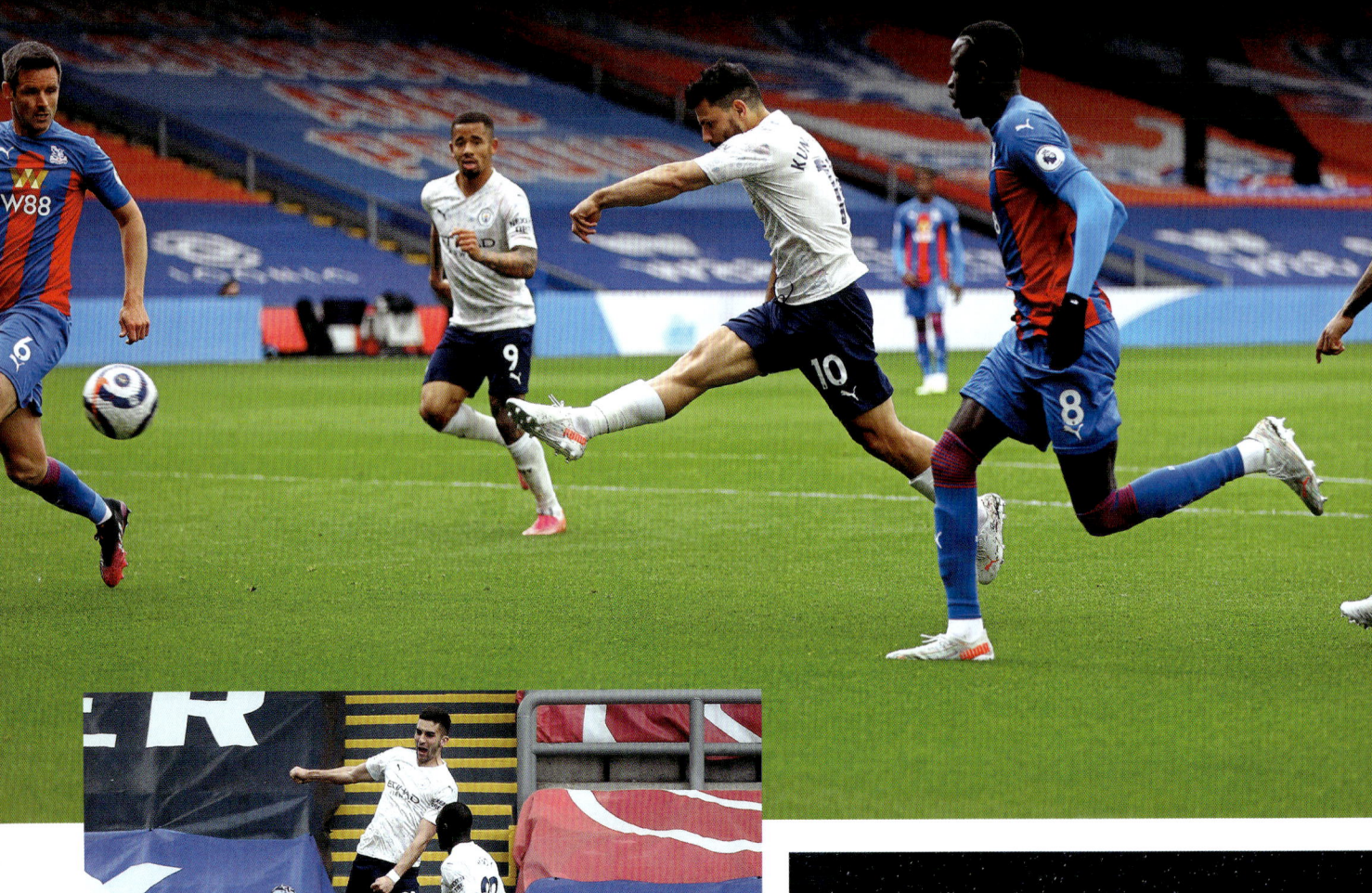

PREMIER LEAGUE CHAMPIONS 20/21

78 www.mancity.com

# MAY

GOALS from Sergio Aguero and Ferran Torres moved City to within two points of regaining the Premier League title as we secured an impressive 2-0 victory at Crystal Palace at the start of the month.

Second half strikes from record scorer Aguero – his 258th for the Club – and Torres were enough to earn us an incredible 19th successive away victory in all competitions and a record-equalling 11th straight win in the Premier League.

The win moved us 13 points clear at the top of the table with four games remaining and brought up 700 goals for City during Pep Guardiola's time in charge.

The following Tuesday, and it was Riyad Mahrez's turn to star as the Algerian scored twice against 10-man Paris Saint-Germain to send us through to the Champions League final for the first time with a 4-1 aggregate victory.

## WE DID IT. WE MADE AN INCREDIBLE CHAMPIONS LEAGUE SEASON AND NOW DESERVE TO BE THERE IN THE FINAL

**PEP GUARDIOLA**

---

14.05.21
St James' Park, Premier League

**NEWCASTLE UNITED**     **3**
Krafth (25) Joelinton (45'+6 pen) Willock (62)

**MAN CITY**     **4**
Cancelo (39) Torres (42, 64, 66)

---

18.05.21
AMEX Stadium, Premier League

**BRIGHTON & HOVE ALBION**     **3**
Trossard (50) Webster (72) Burn (76)

**MAN CITY**     **2**
Gündogan (2) Foden (48)

---

23.05.21
Etihad Stadium, Premier League

**MAN CITY**     **5**
De Bruyne (11) Jesus (14) Foden (53) Aguero (71, 76)

**EVERTON**     **0**

---

29.05.21
Estádio do Dragão, Porto, Portugal, Champions League Final

**MAN CITY**     **0**

**CHELSEA**     **1**
Havertz (42)

www.mancity.com 79

PREMIER LEAGUE CHAMPIONS 20/21

Having seized control of the tie with a superb performance in the first leg, Guardiola's side delivered another outstanding display, with Mahrez again the match winner.

Having helped us tighten our grip on the contest in just the 11th minute when he reacted quickest to Kevin De Bruyne's deflected shot to slide the ball under Keylor Navas, the winger put the result beyond doubt just after the hour as he tapped in Phil Foden's cross at the far post to finish off a slick counter-attacking move.

Our hopes of being crowned Premier League champions in the next game were frustrated, however, as we lost out 2-1 at home to Chelsea.

Knowing victory would see us regain the title, we secured a 44th minute lead thanks to Raheem Sterling's close-range strike.

Sergio Aguero then saw a 45th minute penalty saved – and Chelsea hit back after the break as Hakim Ziyech levelled affairs on the hour.

And as we strove to find a winner, it was Chelsea who emerged triumphant, Marcos Alonso beating Ederson in injury time to seal the victory and ensure our wait to be crowned champions went on.

> I FLICKED THE BALL, AND I THINK IT WAS A VERY BEAUTIFUL GOAL! IT'S BEEN AN INCREDIBLE WEEK, WE QUALIFY FOR THE CHAMPIONS LEAGUE FINAL, WIN THE PREMIER LEAGUE AND THEN I SCORE A HAT-TRICK, I AM VERY HAPPY.
>
> **FERRAN TORRES**

MAY

The title was secured the following Tuesday – and we didn't even have to kick a ball. Manchester United's defeat at the hands of Leicester City meant we couldn't be caught, so we travelled to Newcastle that Friday night as champions once again.

And the game did not disappoint. Ferran Torres hit a 22-minute hat-trick – including a sumptuously back-heeled effort into the far corner, which would go on to win the Nissan Goal of the Season – following Joao Cancelo's opener as we edged an absorbing seven-goal thriller against the Magpies.

Newcastle led, then trailed, then led again before the Champions hit back in a match that will be regarded as a Premier League classic.

The victory also set a new English record of 12 successive away victories in the league.

And that is where the record stands after we saw a two-goal lead wiped out by a resurgent Brighton, who recovered to win 3-2 in our penultimate league game of the season.

Joao Cancelo was red carded after just 10 minutes, but goals from Ilkay Gundogan and Phil Foden looked to have put City on the way to a 13th Premier League away win in succession.

The Seagulls, buoyed by a passionate home crowd, eventually made the extra man count with three second half goals to secure a first top flight victory over City for 40 years.

www.mancity.com 81

**PREMIER LEAGUE CHAMPIONS 20/21**

But the Champions produced a dazzling display in front of 10,000 fans on our return to the Etihad for our final league game of the season, as a double from Sergio Aguero and goals from Kevin De Bruyne, Gabriel Jesus and Phil Foden secured a dominant 5-0 victory over Everton.

De Bruyne started the rout in the first-half with Jesus quickly adding another to set the tone for the lucky fans in attendance.

Golden Gloves winner Ederson helped secure his 19th clean sheet of the season with a first half penalty save from Gylfi Sigurdsson, and it took us just eight second-half minutes to add a deserved third through Foden.

And then it was all eyes on a magical Aguero cameo as he finished with the outside of his boot to make it 4-0 just eight minutes after coming on, before five minutes later soaring to head home Fernandinho's superb cross to make it 5-0, in the process overtaking Wayne Rooney as the player to score the most Premier League goals for a single club. Talk about fairy tales.

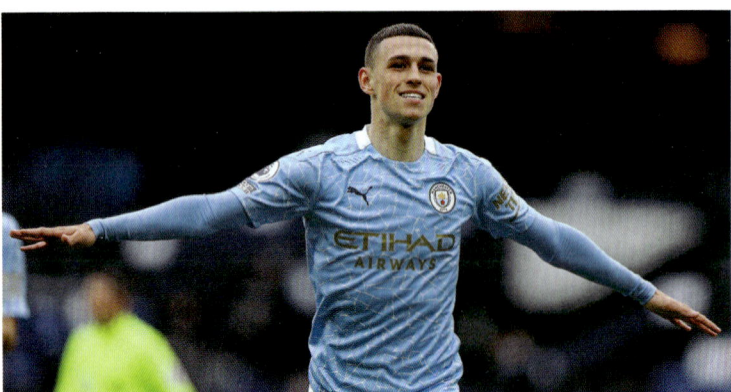

But not all fairy tales have a happy ending. City's first Champions League final, switched from Istanbul to Porto, finished in a 1-0 defeat to Chelsea.

Kai Havertz opened the scoring for Chelsea and just when City were looking like getting back into it, skipper Kevin De Bruyne was forced off with an acute fracture of the nose and an orbital fracture to his left eye socket following a challenge by Antonio Rudiger.

"We showed courage, especially in the second half," reflected Pep Guardiola at full-time in Estadio do Dragao. "I just want to congratulate the players for an exceptional season and the game they played today."

# DIAS NAMED ETIHAD PLAYER OF THE SEASON

**Ruben Dias is Manchester City's 2020/21 Etihad Airways Player of the Season.**

The Portuguese centre-back, who was also named the 2021 Football Writers' Association Footballer of the Year, has enjoyed a dream debut campaign, playing a crucial role in City's success.

The 24-year-old – signed from Benfica last summer – has been an integral cog in Pep Guardiola's relentless, record-breaking machine, clocking 49 appearances and scoring two goals.

In addition to lifting the Premier League trophy and our fourth successive Carabao Cup, Dias has also been key in our Champions League campaign. Since falling behind in our opening day win over Porto, City did not concede another goal until the quarter-final stage and kept another clean sheet in the last four second leg triumph over Paris Saint-Germain.

Asked how it felt to have won the award in his debut season, Dias expressed his gratitude to his teammates.

"I'm very pleased but I won't let go the fact that I'm only here receiving this because we won the Premier League, the Carabao Cup and we're in the Final of the Champions League," he declared.

"Big credit goes to my teammates, especially because I'm a defender. For a defender to win this, it's mainly because of the team. Big thanks to all of my teammates.

"For a kid that before all of it was a fan and dreamed of becoming one of the stars, I am really happy to be here and to have the opportunity to play with all the guys I play with in my team."

PREMIER LEAGUE CHAMPIONS 20/21

# Picture Perfect

**HERE is the full story of our season – in pictures.**

Featuring everything from behind-the-scenes during the COVID-19 pandemic to the snow in May, our three Premier League Champions and our Women's FA Cup-winners, this is how our award-winning Photography Team of Victoria Haydn, Matt McNulty and Tom Flathers saw things unfurl in a season like no other.

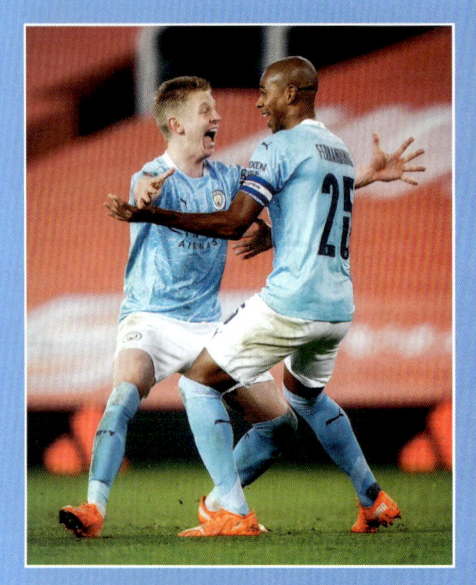

84 www.mancity.com

PICTURE PERFECT

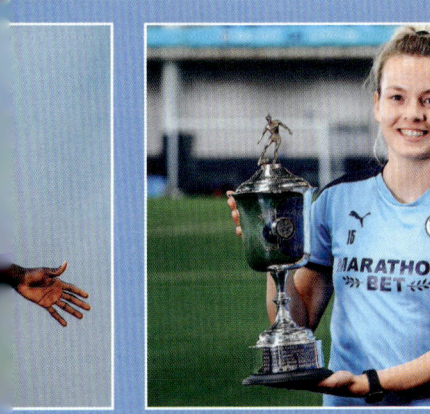

www.mancity.com 85

**PREMIER LEAGUE CHAMPIONS 20/21**

86 www.mancity.com

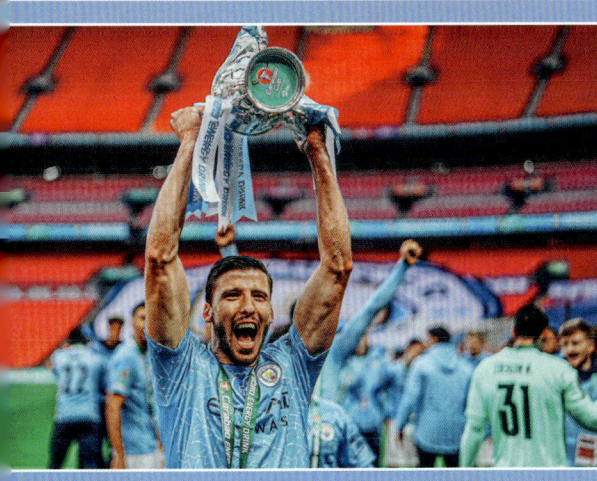

PICTURE PERFECT

www.mancity.com 87

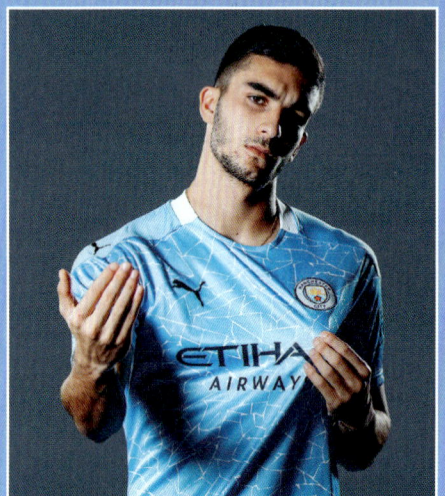

**PREMIER LEAGUE CHAMPIONS 20/21**

88 www.mancity.com

PICTURE PERFECT

www.mancity.com 89

**PREMIER LEAGUE CHAMPIONS 20/21**

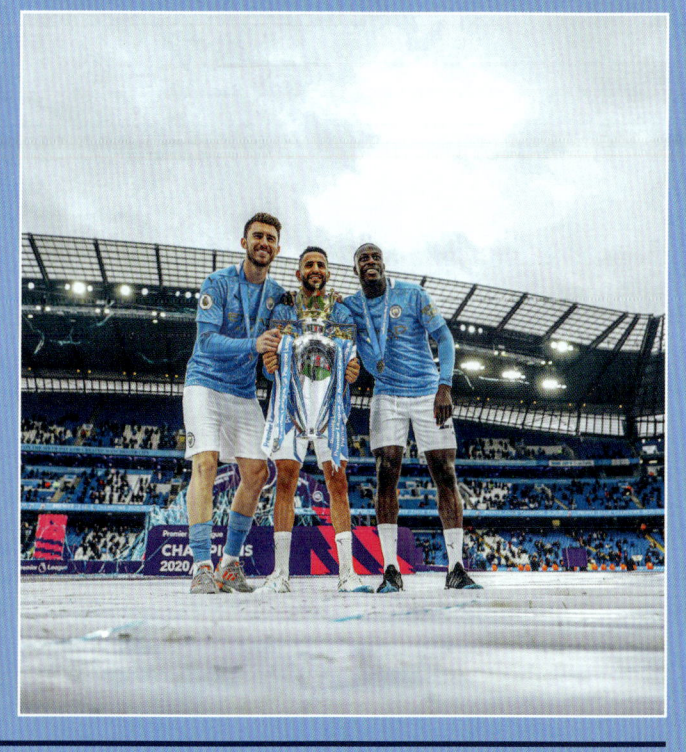

PICTURE PERFECT

www.mancity.com 91

# X3 PREMIER LEAGUE CHAMPIONS 2020/21

# EDS & ACADEMY

**IT has been a superb season for City's Academy teams. Here, Neil Leigh takes a look back at a memorable campaign.**

Ahead of the 2010/21 season there was a new look to both the EDS and Under-18 coaching set-ups.

Enzo Maresca was appointed to the role of EDS Head Coach in late August with Danny Walker stepping into the position of assistant head coach.

And with Gareth Taylor moving to take charge of our women's team, Carlos Vicens was installed as Head Coach for our Under-18s during the summer of 2020, having previously worked as assistant to Gareth at Under-18 level.

Marseca and Vicens quickly made their mark with both our EDS and Under-18s squads hitting the ground running, impressing not only with results but - just as significantly - with the manner in which that on-field success was achieved.

Resuming the 2019/20 FA Cup Youth Cup campaign, which had been put on hiatus for six months due to the COVID-19 pandemic, Vicens' Under-18s lifted the trophy in memorable fashion in early November of 2020.

Having overcome Blackburn Rovers in the semi-final, City then lifted the FA Youth Cup for the third time in our history with a thrilling 3-2 victory over Chelsea in an enthralling encounter at St George's Park, Cole Palmer striking the all-important winner.

Palmer along with skipper Tommy Doyle, striker Liam Delap and midfielder James McAtee was also part of a hugely talented group of young players who helped drive our Elite Development Squad to a maiden Premier League title success.

After a spectacular and memorable season, Enzo Maresca's men clinched the title in mid-April and proved worthy winners.

Our EDS side eventually finished a remarkable 14 points clear of nearest rivals Chelsea having chalked up 17 wins, five draws and two losses from our programme.

92 www.mancity.com

**EDS & ACADEMY**

City also plundered 79 goals on the way to the title – 21 more than the next highest scorers Manchester United – and in Delap boasted PL2's leading scorer with the 18-year-old amassing 24 for the season.

Only Everton conceded fewer goals that City's tally of 30 while skipper Tommy Doyle emerged as the leading PL2 assist maker, weighing in with 11 for the season, further proof of the impressive all-round nature of our EDS campaign.

It was a similar tale of success at Under-18 level – though Vicens' squad showed the other side of the Academy's character and mettle, claiming the Under-18 Premier North crown on the final day of the season.

Having been awarded both the Under-18 North and National Premier League titles in the summer of 2020 on a points-per-game basis after the action was suspended in February due to the COVID-19 pandemic, City retained our regional crown in thrilling fashion.

After a titanic tussle with Manchester United, a 1-0 victory at Burnley on May 12 in our final league game was enough to see City be crowned champions once more as we finished a point above United.

Vicens' squad chalked up a magnificent 19 wins, four draws and just one loss across the 20/21 season, scoring 76 goals – only United scored more with 79 – with Tai Sodje second top scorer with a tally of 19.

City's Under-18s also boasted the league's most effective defence, shipping just 19 goals, while Carlos Borges emerged as top assist maker in the Under-18 North programme, contributing 16.

Our reward is a National Final against Under-18 South champions Fulham with the Academy Stadium playing host to the showdown on Saturday, May 22.

www.mancity.com 93

PREMIER LEAGUE CHAMPIONS 20/21

# Record breakers

ALONG the way to securing a third Premier League title in four seasons, City have also accrued a series of outstanding Club and national records.

In what has been the most challenging and demanding of campaigns played against the backdrop of the COVID-19 pandemic, the quality and consistency of Pep Guardiola's squad has garnered widespread praise and admiration.

The continued excellence of City under Pep is further reinforced with the fact that we have now won ten of the past 15 available major English trophies counting from the 2017/18 campaign to today.

Furthermore, the guiding principles of reinvention, resilience and teamwork underpinning the squad, have seen City create a number of new and notable record-breaking achievements along the way to securing a third Premier League crown in four years.

The advent of 2021 saw City establish a new Premier League record for the longest sequence of wins from the start of a calendar year thanks to the 13 league victories we chalked up between January 3 and March 2 of this year.

That formed the centrepiece of a quite remarkable run of 21 consecutive wins in all competitions between December and March which saw City establish another new English top flight record.

City also equalled the Premier League

Manchester City's title is their fifth in the last 10 seasons and since they lifted their first in 2011-12, only Chelsea have won it more than once (2) along with the Sky Blues.

| SEASON | TEAM | MANAGER |
| --- | --- | --- |
| 2011-12 | MANCHESTER CITY | ROBERTO MANCINI |
| 2012-13 | MANCHESTER UNITED | ALEX FERGUSON |
| 2013-14 | MANCHESTER CITY | MANUEL PELLEGRINI |
| 2014-15 | CHELSEA | JOSE MOURINHO |
| 2015-16 | LEICESTER CITY | CLAUDIO RANIERI |
| 2016-17 | CHELSEA | ANTONIO CONTE |
| 2017-18 | MANCHESTER CITY | PEP GUARDIOLA |
| 2018-19 | MANCHESTER CITY | PEP GUARDIOLA |
| 2019-20 | LIVERPOOL | JURGEN KLOPP |
| 2020-21 | MANCHESTER CITY | PEP GUARDIOLA |

record of 19 for the longest run of games without going behind, achieving that distinction between November 28, 2020 and March 2 of this year.

That sustained run of excellence also helped see Pep Guardiola's squad equal our Club record run of 28 games without defeat between November 25, 2020 and March 2, 2021 matching the tally we achieved between April and December in 2017.

City also broke new ground by becoming the first team in the history of the Premier League to be as low as eighth on Christmas Day and then go on to win the title.

## STATS

Manchester City are the first team in the history of the Premier League to be as low as 8th on Christmas Day and then win the title – in top-flight history, only three teams have been lower in the table at Christmas and then won the league, with City themselves the joint-lowest in 1936-37 (12th), also losing 5-3 on Christmas Day to Sheffield Wednesday for their troubles.

| SEASON | POSITION ON CHRISTMAS DAY | TOP FLIGHT WINNERS |
|---|---|---|
| 1936-37 | 12 | MANCHESTER CITY |
| 1981-82 | 12 | LIVERPOOL |
| 1974-75 | 10 | DERBY COUNTY |
| 2020-21 | 8 | MANCHESTER CITY |
| 1912-13 | 7 | SUNDERLAND |
| 1949-59 | 7 | PORTSMOUTH |

In what has proved a season like no other, the records kept on tumbling with City establishing another notable English first by winning all nine of our competitive fixtures in January.

That was the most by a team in the top four tiers of English football in a single month since the formation of the Football League in 1888.

City have also blazed a record-breaking trail on the road.

Our 4-3 win at Newcastle earlier this month saw City establish a new record for consecutive away league wins in the history of the top four tiers of English football.

That victory at St James' Park was our 12th away league win in a row, eclipsing the previous record of 11 held by Chelsea (2008) and ourselves (2017).

It also made it 20 consecutive away wins in all competitions – another record.

The result also saw City go 22 games unbeaten away, yet another Club landmark eclipsing a record the record previously established by Joe Royle's City side between January and September of 1999.

Guardiola's squad are also rewriting the record books on the continent too with our march to the Champions League final seeing us establish several more club firsts.

Our 2-0 win at home to Paris Saint-Germain means saw us set a new club record for our longest unbeaten run in the UEFA Champions League having gone 12 games unbeaten between 21 October, 2020 and 4 May, 2021.

It also saw us set a new record for the longest winning run by an English side in Europe's elite club competition (7).

City are also in the midst of our longest unbeaten home run in the UEFA Champions League, a sequence that now extends for 14 games covering the period from 7 November, 2018 through to 4 May, 2021 (ongoing).

Following a run of five wins in their opening 12 Premier League games, Manchester City then embarked on a 15-match winning run in the competition, only bettered three times in the history of the English top-flight, one of which was by Pep Guardiola's City side back in 2017. They also equalled a 15-game run between February and August 2019, also under Guardiola.

| START OF RUN | END OF RUN | TOP-FLIGHT HISTORY | WINNING RUN |
|---|---|---|---|
| 27/10/2019 | 24/02/2020 | LIVERPOOL | 18 |
| 26/08/2017 | 27/12/2017 | MANCHESTER CITY | 18 |
| 10/03/2019 | 05/10/2019 | LIVERPOOL | 17 |
| 03/02/2019 | 10/08/2019 | MANCHESTER CITY | 15 |
| 19/12/2020 | 02/03/2021 | MANCHESTER CITY | 15 |

PREMIER LEAGUE CHAMPIONS 20/21

Pep Guardiola

## PEP GUARDIOLA RECORD BREAKER

### Pep Guardiola Player stats

| DATE OF BIRTH | PLACE OF BIRTH | POSITION AS A PLAYER | DEBUT AS A PLAYER |
|---|---|---|---|
| 18 JANUARY 1971 | SANTPEDOR, SPAIN | DEFENSIVE MIDFIELDER | v CADIZ SPANISH LA LIGA 16.12.90 |

#### TEAMS PLAYED FOR AS A PLAYER

| YEARS | TEAM | APPEARANCES | GOALS |
|---|---|---|---|
| 1990–2001 | BARCELONA, SPAIN | 263 | 6 |
| 2001–2002 | BRESCIA, ITALY | 11 | 2 |
| 2002–2003 | ROMA, ITALY | 4 | 0 |
| 2003 | BRESCIA, ITALY | 13 | 1 |
| 2003–2005 | AL-AHLI, QATAR | 36 | 5 |
| 2005-2006 | DORADOS, MEXICO | 10 | 1 |

#### NATIONAL TEAM

| 1991 | SPAIN U21 | 2 | 0 |
|---|---|---|---|
| 1991-92 | SPAIN U23 | 12 | 2 |
| 1992-2001 | SPAIN | 47 | 5 |

### Pep Guardiola Manager stats

#### TEAMS MANAGED

| YEARS | TEAM | GAMES | APPOINTED |
|---|---|---|---|
| 2008–2012 | BARCELONA, SPAIN | 247 | 1 JULY, 2008 |
| 2013–2016 | BAYERN MUNICH, GERMANY | 161 | 1 JULY 2013 |
| 2016 | MANCHESTER CITY | 292 on going | 1 JULY, 2016 |

Guardiola has now won the title in nine of his 12 seasons managing in the top-flight, winning exactly three titles with each of Barcelona, Bayern Munich and Manchester City.

| CLUB | SEASON | GAMES | WON | DRAWN | LOST | GOALS FOR | GOALS AGAINST | POINTS | FINAL POSITION |
|---|---|---|---|---|---|---|---|---|---|
| BARCELONA | 2008-09 | 38 | 27 | 6 | 5 | 105 | 35 | 87 | 1 |
| BARCELONA | 2009-10 | 38 | 31 | 6 | 1 | 98 | 24 | 99 | 1 |
| BARCELONA | 2010-11 | 38 | 30 | 6 | 2 | 95 | 21 | 96 | 1 |
| BARCELONA | 2011-12 | 38 | 28 | 7 | 3 | 114 | 29 | 91 | 2 |
| FC BAYERN MUNICH | 2013-14 | 34 | 29 | 3 | 2 | 94 | 23 | 90 | 1 |
| FC BAYERN MUNICH | 2014-15 | 34 | 25 | 4 | 5 | 80 | 18 | 79 | 1 |
| FC BAYERN MUNICH | 2015-16 | 34 | 28 | 4 | 2 | 80 | 17 | 88 | 1 |
| MANCHESTER CITY | 2016-17 | 38 | 23 | 9 | 6 | 80 | 39 | 78 | 3 |
| MANCHESTER CITY | 2017-18 | 38 | 32 | 4 | 2 | 106 | 27 | 100 | 1 |
| MANCHESTER CITY | 2018-19 | 38 | 32 | 2 | 4 | 95 | 23 | 98 | 1 |
| MANCHESTER CITY | 2019-20 | 38 | 26 | 3 | 9 | 102 | 35 | 81 | 2 |
| MANCHESTER CITY | 2020-21 | 38 | 27 | 5 | 6 | 83 | 32 | 86 | 1 |

Pep Guardiola has secured his third English top-flight title and is one of only four managers to win as many as three Premier League titles, along with Sir Alex Ferguson (13), Arsene Wenger and Jose Mourinho (3 each).

| MANAGER | PREMIER LEAGUE CHAMPION | SEASONS |
|---|---|---|
| ALEX FERGUSON | 13 | 1992-93, 1993-94, 1995-96, 1996-97, 1998-99, 1999-00, 2000-01, 2002-03, 2006-07, 2007-08, 2008-09, 2010-11, 2012-13 |
| ARSÈNE WENGER | 3 | 1997-98, 2001-02, 2003-04 |
| JOSÉ MOURINHO | 3 | 2004-05, 2005-06, 2014-15 |
| PEP GUARDIOLA | 3 | 2017-18, 2018-19, 2020-21 |
| KENNY DALGLISH | 1 | 1994-95 |
| CARLO ANCELOTTI | 1 | 2009-10 |
| ROBERTO MANCINI | 1 | 2011-12 |
| MANUEL PELLEGRINI | 1 | 2013-14 |
| CLAUDIO RANIERI | 1 | 2015-16 |
| ANTONIO CONTE | 1 | 2016-17 |
| JÜRGEN KLOPP | 1 | 2019-20 |

Pep Guardiola is only the fourth manager to win as many as three English top-flight titles in his first five seasons managing in the competition, after Tom Watson (Sunderland), Bob Paisley (Liverpool) and Kenny Dalglish (Liverpool).

| MANAGER | CLUB |
|---|---|
| PEP GUARDIOLA | 3 |
| BOB PAISLEY | 3 |
| KENNY DALGLISH | 3 |
| TOM WATSON | 3 |
| BILL SHANKLY | 2 |
| BOB JACKSON | 2 |
| GEORGE ALLISON | 2 |
| GEORGE GRAHAM | 2 |
| HERBERT CHAPMAN | 2 |
| JOSÉ MOURINHO | 2 |
| ROBERT BROWN | 2 |

Guardiola becomes one of only 12 managers in English top-flight history to win the title as many as three times.

| MANAGER | TOP-FLIGHT TITLES | CLUB |
|---|---|---|
| ALEX FERGUSON | 13 | MANCHESTER UNITED |
| BOB PAISLEY | 6 | LIVERPOOL |
| GEORGE RAMSAY | 6 | ASTON VILLA |
| MATT BUSBY | 5 | MANCHESTER UNITED |
| TOM WATSON | 5 | SUNDERLAND, LIVERPOOL |
| HERBERT CHAPMAN | 4 | HUDDERSFIELD TOWN, ARSENAL |
| KENNY DALGLISH | 4 | LIVERPOOL, BLACKBURN ROVERS |
| PEP GUARDIOLA | 3 | MANCHESTER CITY |
| ARSENE WENGER | 3 | ARSENAL |
| BILL SHANKLY | 3 | LIVERPOOL |
| JOSÉ MOURINHO | 3 | CHELSEA |
| STAN CULLIS | 3 | WOLVERHAMPTON WANDERERS |

## WHAT THEY SAID

**WINNING THE PREMIER LEAGUE IS THE ULTIMATE FULFILMENT OF OUR AMBITIONS. IT'S WHAT WE ALL DREAMED OF AS YOUNG PLAYERS, SO TO DO IT IS A WONDERFUL FEELING**

FERNANDINHO

**THIS HAS BEEN A SEASON AND A PREMIER LEAGUE TITLE LIKE NO OTHER. THIS WAS THE HARDEST ONE. WE WILL ALWAYS REMEMBER THIS SEASON FOR THE WAY THAT WE WON. I AM SO PROUD TO BE THE MANAGER HERE AND OF THIS GROUP OF PLAYERS**

PEP GUARDIOLA

**TO WIN MY FIRST PREMIER LEAGUE IS SOMETHING THAT EVERY PLAYER DREAMS OF. WE WERE ALL VERY HAPPY, BOTH ME AND MY FAMILY. IT MEANS A LOT WINNING THE PREMIER LEAGUE, ESPECIALLY IN MY FIRST YEAR HERE. IT'S BEEN THE RESULT OF A LOT OF HARD WORK THROUGHOUT THE WHOLE SEASON. WE GOT THE REWARD OF WINNING THE CARABAO CUP FIRST AND NOW THE PREMIER LEAGUE**

FERRAN TORRES

**BIG TROPHIES, YOU ONLY WIN WITH BIG TEAMS. OF COURSE WE ARE TEAMMATES BUT WE ARE MORE THAN THAT, WE ARE FRIENDS. WE ALMOST LIVE THE SAME LIFE AS A SECOND FAMILY. IT'S A CELEBRATION OF THIS SUCCESS OF THE HARD WORK. EVERYONE HAS TAKEN PART AND RESPONSIBILITY OF THIS**

RODRIGO

**WHAT HAPPENED THIS SEASON, WITH COVID, THE RESTRICTIONS, WE COULDN'T ENJOY NORMAL LIFE, LIKE EVERYONE IN THE WORLD, OF COURSE. BUT IT MAKES IT EVEN MORE DIFFICULT. TO COME BACK FROM LAST SEASON'S CHAMPIONS LEAGUE, NO HOLIDAYS, INJURIES, COVID…AND WHAT THIS TEAM HAS DONE HAS BEEN INCREDIBLE. THE PLAYERS, COACH, FOOTBALL CLUB, FANS AND THERE IS A TOGETHERNESS THAT MAKES US SPECIAL**

DIRECTOR OF FOOTBALL TXIKI BEGIRISTAIN

**I JUST FEEL REALLY LUCKY. WE HAVE SO MANY GREAT PLAYERS. I GREW UP DREAMING TO BE IN THIS TEAM AND IT'S JUST SO SPECIAL FOR ME. SOMETIMES I JUST SIT THERE AND THINK ABOUT IT [WINNING SILVERWARE]. WE'RE GOING IN THE RIGHT DIRECTION AND HOPEFULLY WE WILL WIN MORE TITLES AND BE MORE SUCCESSFUL**

PHIL FODEN

**IT'S BEEN A SPECIAL ONE. THE FIRST TITLE WAS GREAT TO GET OVER THE LINE BUT THE FEELING DOESN'T GET OLD WHEN YOU'RE UP THERE AND LIFTING THE TROPHY**

KYLE WALKER

**TO HAVE ACHIEVED WHAT WE HAVE IN THIS SEASON IS INCREDIBLE. IN THESE TIMES WITH COVID WITH GAMES EVERY THREE DAYS IT SHOULDN'T BE UNDERESTIMATED. EVERYONE HAS COME TOGETHER AS ONE AND I'M REALLY PROUD OF EVERY SINGLE ONE OF THE PEOPLE HERE**

JOHN STONES

**I WANT TO THANK MY TEAMMATES BECAUSE THEY HAVE HELPED A LOT. THANK YOU FOR EVERYTHING. I'M SO HAPPY BECAUSE IT'S NOT EASY TO BE TEN YEARS AT ONE CLUB. SO FOR ME IT'S AN HONOUR**

SERGIO AGUERO